Bricks and Mortar
for Educational Reform

Muriel Wasi

Foreword by
Krishna Kumar

First Published 2021
(incorporating Bricks and Mortar, 1964;
Transition 1971; Living and Learning 1978)

ISBN 978–93–83723–67–6

Published by
LG PUBLISHERS DISTRIBUTORS
49, Street No. 14, Pratap Nagar
Mayur Vihar Phase I, Delhi 110091
lgpdist@gmail.com

Typeset at
Limited Colors, Delhi

Printed at
D.K. Fine Art Press, Delhi

Contents

Foreword

Despite the passage of time since these essays were written, they feel fresh and relevant. The feeling of freshness can be attributed to the author's style, but what about relevance? It is indeed rare for a commentary on the system of education written more than half a century ago to offer insights that might be useful today. The reason why Muriel Wasi's reflections on schooling and childhood in India are relevant today is not that the system has remained inert. In its own ways and at its own pace, the system has changed just as India and its society have. Muriel Wasi continues to be worthy of attention because her voice is authentic and rooted in deep understanding—of education as well as of India.

Muriel Wasi's writing reminds us of an era when our Republic was young. Its priorities had been sharply articulated in the Constitution. The challenge these priorities posed to education was well understood and accepted. It was widely believed that the transformative vision codified in the Constitution called for urgent reforms in education. Resources were scarce and the system of education was stuck in colonial and pre-colonial legacies. As we go through Muriel Wasi's essays, we recognise a mind anguished and excited at the same time. Her style combines elegance with clarity and conviction—a mixture that permits her to criticise entrenched vested interests and the institutional structures that serve these interests. Similarly, her passion and concern go together. This combination enabled her to draw upon a wide range of thought and experience from around the world. Her sustained engagement with history and psychology, literature and aesthetics gave her a distinctive vision to spot systemic flaws and institutional weaknesses that encourage orthodoxy and inertia.

Reading Muriel Wasi in the present moment reassures our disturbed minds. At a time when the humanities are losing ground in an increasingly instrumentalist advisory landscape, Wasi's words help us to guard against loss of perspective. The essays included in this volume cover diverse themes, such as curriculum and pedagogy, adolescence and youth, language and theatre. Shorter comments are included along with papers written for formal occasions. The volume gives us the privilege of meeting a woman in whose personality administrative judgement and experience was enriched by pedagogic subtlety and theoretical awareness. We miss such a colleague today: this volume compensates for her absence to the extent books can do such a thing.

She reminds us of fundamentals, such as the relationship between political values reflected in the Constitution and learning at school; the distinctive role of teachers in the maintenance of liberal democracy. Her vocabulary may be different, but we can sense what she is getting at. One doesn't always agree with her, at times because we have the benefit of hindsight, but she is always reminding the reader that disagreement is the first step towards progress. She is a practitioner of democracy, both in substance and style. Her patient, persuasive analysis of complex issues reminds us that educational reform necessarily involves prolonged quarrels.

The pleasure we derive from her writing can hardly be attributed to the nostalgia it evokes. It has more to do with the realisation that listening to older advice might be one source of stamina we need in order to cope with the current crises. We are so lost in the digital din of our times that the past seems irrelevant. Some voices go so far as to condemn earlier planners and policies. Muriel Wasi's renewed presence will steady our minds in the turbulent atmosphere in which we live.

Krishna Kumar
former Director, NCERT

Memoriam

It was the summer of 1972 and we had just entered our second year at Jesus & Mary College. The excitement and challenge of moving from school to college had ebbed a little. Our first year results under our belts, it was too early to start working for the next set of examinations. We knew our way around college, the shortest route to Chanakya Theatre and Fujiya Restaurant; we were, in truth, somewhat bored. A new teacher had been appointed to take us through the plays of William Shakespeare; her name was Muriel Wasi.

From Mrs Wasi's first encounter with our class it was apparent that she fully intended to exceed her brief as Shakespeare became only one of the things she taught us. Each text that she lectured on ('worked on together' was her phrase) opened up vistas of discussions on all the issues that were relevant to 18 year-old minds. By our third year, she had performed a miracle of sorts—she had organized a group of us into a 'library seminar' where we actually read books not on our syllabus (unheard of) and stayed back for hours after college ended to discuss them.

Our association did not end with my graduation from Jesus & Mary College. I then travelled to Trinity College in Dublin to study further. Before I reached my destination, a letter from Mrs Wasi awaited me, full of sound advice and tips that she could have conveyed to me earlier, but which she saw would have greater meaning in my new environment. Over the years, Mrs Wasi never gave up on her former students, sometimes taking more trouble than we did ourselves to ensure that we kept in touch with each other. She would arrange meetings at which we sometimes met each other, occasionally new people, and always new ideas.

Mrs Wasi showed us, her students, that Literature was a vehicle for ideas. She spotted potential in her students by moving beyond our own self-assessment or surface judgements, which is what made her such an exceptional pedagogue, and such a dearly loved teacher. So, for forty years, I myself gave lectures at Jesus & Mary College, always hoping to carry back into the classroom something of what she brought into it for us.

It is very exciting to have a chance to hear Mrs Wasi's voice once again, in the form of these essays. Written decades ago, they are indubitably topical today, as they speak directly to problems in secondary school education. In the opening essay, Mrs Wasi sets out lucidly the need to *sustain* the standard of quality teachers, the relationship that a Principal has to the staff and students of an institution, and the requirement for "bricks and mortar" which cannot be replaced with "teaching under the trees," sometimes mistaken for a revivalist and nationalist alternative. As she steps into the minefield of the use of the English language as a medium of instruction, the writer clarifies that she is talking not of the English Literature of postgraduate studies, but the language used for the teaching of science and the humanities, a choice that ideally should not be coloured by partisan lens. When looking at the teaching of history in school, she argues that it cannot rightfully be separated from the study of geography. Even more challenging are the essays that deal with Leadership, Freedom, and Authority, all terms as open to debate today as they were in the 1960s. The vexed question of how to evaluate the correct allocation of scholarships in a country as large and diverse as India takes up another essay. And an absolute gem is the chapter that deals with the institution of schooling in the form of a fable, told as an exchange of letters. Every essay in this collection is packed with insight regarding the inexhaustible subject of education as it is, and as it should be. Together the collection makes absorbing reading for anyone who has been even remotely touched by the speculative question of education.

Jayanti Kaul

former Professor of English, Jesus & Mary College

Introduction

Bricks and Mortar is an insightful treatise on education encompassing many of its dimensions, from the conceptual to the practical in the contexts of teaching-learning processes and the learning outcomes. Though most of the pieces in this anthology are presumably written in the decades of the 1970s and 80s, they are of great contemporary relevance. It touches on almost every pertinent issue relating to education that we are still engaged with in the current times.

The author brings both an objective and subjective perspective to the anthology based on her vast experience in the field of education including 18 years of her experience in educational planning and administration at the governmental level followed by her teaching experience in two prominent colleges of the University of Delhi. Thus her essays straddle across the domain of education both at the school and college levels.

Muriel Wasi examines the fundamentals that constitute 'good education' in its many dimensions through the metaphor of 'bricks and mortar'. Beginning with good buildings and good surroundings, good teachers who are essential teachers, educational leadership, sensitive teaching-learning processes, and the pursuit of excellence lie at the core of good education. The essence of good education implies the imparting of educational values without losing sight of the traditional values of a society and the shared values of a country while promoting a fundamentally critical and enquiring mind on the lines of the Socratic examined life. She catches the note of the coming age in her examination of the role that technology could play in making the educational opportunities more accessible and equitable, a highly pertinent issue in the present times of the pandemic and exploration of the viability of online learning methods. She rightly views education as a single most potent instrument of change and that good education should therefore empower the student leading to capacity building rather than merely increasing knowledge. Without losing sight of the core values of democracy and equity education in India has got to be innovative in view of its diversity where a typical standardised school is not possible. On the whole it is not enough to have educated individuals but education must inculcate social responsibility and develop social conscience.

A whole range of issues that are still pertinent in the educational sphere in the current times are incisively examined in the anthology. Teaching of languages and in particular teaching of the English language, the complexity of translation of plays have not lost their relevance for those engaged in teaching and research in the languages. With the emphasis on professional education in the current times, the importance of teaching and learning humanities in the colleges, and the need for a multidisciplinary approach in teaching examined by the author can hardly be ignored.

Issues relating to formal and non-formal education, mechanisms of making education accessible to the less privileged, elitism of public schools are all issues still pertinent. Whether scholarships should be merit-based or means-based driven by the concern for equity is carefully examined in that context. The author's all round approach to education is evident when she turns her attention to the Library as an invaluable learning resource and indispensable to education. In this context the issue of the state of libraries does not escape her attention. The progress of educational publications from official pamphlets and handouts to more comprehensive issues related to education has also received due attention in this comprehensive volume.

What makes people associate universities like Oxford and Cambridge with excellence? The author opines that emphasis on promoting scholarship and training of the mind with truth and integrity are the core features of such good institutions. The quality of good institutions lies in developing in the students 'a code of thinking and living with truth and integrity that leads to an ethic for living an honourable life, an attitude of mind and spirit'.

I would recommend this anthology to all those interested and engaged in the theory and practice of education at various levels.

Malathi Subramanian
former Principal, Daulat Ram College,
University of Delhi

1

Bricks and Mortar

I

A socialist in a forgotten novel, *South Riding*, by Winifred Holtby, says: "I believe in bricks and mortar."

He means a good deal more. He means that there can be no good education without good secondary schools; that there can be no good secondary schools without good buildings; that there can be no good buildings without good bricks and mortar.

A few days ago someone said that schools in tents are uncomfortable in a Delhi winter. They should be uncomfortable in all weathers in all parts of any progressive country. For, schools were no more intended to be run in tents than they were intended to be run in the rustic simplicity of revivalist education under trees. Only when you cannot pay for bricks and mortar should you think about tents and trees. But not till then.

And what you can pay for secondary schools depends on how important you think secondary schools are to the making of the Indian nation. One reason for failure, and not the least important reason, is bad or inefficient schooling. Bad or inefficient schooling is directly related to many things, but one of these things is incontrovertibly bricks and mortar, the sheer business of building and building sensibly, not to pattern or model, foreign or native, but to a need, relevant, urgent, present-day.

One of the superstitions on which what I have called "revivalist education" (that sometimes mistakes itself for patriotic, national education) bases itself is that it does not matter much what your school looks or feels like if you have good teachers. But a school is more than an idea. A school is a fact, a physical fact. It is intended to cater not for an isolated genius who can live down his surroundings in a glow of ideas, but for a group of ordinary people, some young, some middle-aged, who are responsive to their immediate environment.

A school is also a social fact that cannot be overlooked. Even good teachers, teachers by choice and vocation, are apt to be impressed by classrooms and buildings that do not have to apologise for themselves. For even dedicated teachers, perhaps especially dedicated teachers, understand that good teaching in the long run, and by habit, is possible only in rooms and surroundings that sustain inspiration, encourage the interchange of thought and confer that "sense of the meeting" that makes bodies such as the Quakers a compact brotherhood.

Good schooling is directly related to good classrooms. Good classrooms are a function of space and sunlight, and sensible furnishing. They need not and should not provide for relaxation; they must provide for comfort adequate to learning with enjoyment. There is no conflict between instruction and enjoyment if classrooms are adequately equipped. The notion that instruction to be remembered must be administered in discomfort is purely masochistic and dated. We must not make a virtue of either poverty or austerity. Neither is in itself good.

"When Sir John Sargent was in India in 1961-62 at the invitation of the Government of West Bengal, he was asked to report on the schools of the state. He did so. Recalling his impressions at a meeting later, he mentioned that it was of some importance that schools should be made to look attractive. A pretty school is the first step to a good school. Mark that. It is not the last, but the first step, for evidently there are things more vital to good secondary education than bricks and mortar. The point is that these things can be added to us only after we have bricks and mortar.

Some years ago I visited the Philippines and was taken round that household word of Filipino education—the Community School. It was an invitation to Indian educationists to think again. It was housed in a gaily-coloured building, with a frontage of brightly-coloured flower-pots, neat lawns and tall trees. There was about it a liberating sense of space that is so necessary for growing children, and a sense of light that is so necessary for growing minds. The children had every aid to enjoyment including a personality corner fitted with dressing table and mirror (with washing equipment) in which they could, without fear of prudery or rebuke, see that they were neat, clean and pretty. They were. They were not more intelligent than Indian children, perhaps they were less well-informed, but they enjoyed themselves. Work in school was stimulating, something to think about, laugh about, live for. The teachers were young, happy-looking, not weighed down with the cares of years, and poverty and humiliation. There was comradeship, an awareness of beauty in surroundings as an integral part—undiscussed because assumed—of education.

They were called Community Schools because the community had in them a constant, physical, economic sense of participation. As a community is proud of its health services, so, it seems, a community may legitimately be proud of its educational services. For, the mind and the body of a people are not so easily demarcated in a progressive society.

The community maintained the school. "With this stake in it, parents took care to see that their children's attendance at school was regular, that their clothes were clean, that they developed a sense of responsibility for the school's cleanliness. They did not break or damage the furniture; furniture was communal property. They did not throw litter about the garden; the garden was understood to be a place for flowers and greenery, not for banana skins, orange peel, and paper. The children were citizens in the making. That is what happens when a community participates in the raising and maintenance of brick-and-mortar schools.

There was a time, and that before 1947, when we could afford nebulously to say: "Let the government attend to it." This is no longer sensible. If the schools that our children must go to are non-existent, i.e. exist in tents or trees, it is the business of parents to see that buildings go up. It is the business of the community to see that specialists in school architecture advise on such matters as light, ventilation, sanitation and acoustics, on classrooms, commonrooms, auditoria, corridors, refectories, playgrounds, hostel facilities and parking space.

It is the business of the community to ensure that those willing and able to put up schools and keep them going in accordance with the highest standards of secondary education are allowed to do so. Only the community can, by the pressure of its indignation and the promise of unwavering scrutiny, create and keep such schools in being. And the community must insist not only on bricks and mortar but on the efficient use of both.

Efficiency implies beauty. A pretty school is the first step to a good school. Bricks and mortar are only a first step, but a necessary first step to good secondary education.

II

A good secondary school is a function of many things, and the first of them bricks and mortar efficiently used for the needs of a progressive country. Bricks and mortar are a literal and primary necessity for good secondary education.

But they are more than a literal necessity; they are a composite and symbolic necessity. For, they attract good communities of teachers and students, and a good secondary school needs both good teachers and good students.

Good teachers are neither born nor made overnight. Conversely, neither God nor teacher-training establishments can be blamed for bad teachers. A good teacher is the product of a good and sensible society. God makes him or her. A teacher-training establishment seeks to improve him or her. But only a good school of good brick and mortar can, with various added implications, keep good teachers good.

What elements cohere and jump to make and keep teachers good? The first is always a simple, physical ingredient, for the teacher is as much the product of a healthy body and mind as is the artist or the administrator. The teacher is a creature of environment. Environment stretches over a responsive childhood and youth, but even more over an adult professional teaching life. It is this last period for which teachers have to be guaranteed good working conditions.

An adequate salary is important to a teacher because it sustains, stimulates, enthuses, confers status and offers leisure that, by a process of rejuvenation, makes and keeps him receptive. A salary is not, however, the last word. A teacher who takes a job solely on its emoluments is making a rash decision. More important than a pay-packet is the working conditions in which he teaches mathematics, she teaches history, they teach art.

What are these determining conditions? First, bricks and mortar skilfully used to make a good, modern, healthy, well-ventilated and functionally-inspiring arena of service. Next, the atmosphere that is created by wise administration. And this is as real, though not as tangible, as bricks and mortar.

For, a teacher more than most people is apt to be permanently and acutely aware of atmosphere. The fact that this is partly of her own making (I use the sex most appropriate to each context) she may overlook, but she knows that it exists, here, round her, in her, among the children she educates. Not all of this stems from a principal, but most of it does from a relationship between principal and staff, and from inter-staff relationships. Somewhere between the extremes of educational exuberance and educational lethargy is a zone of practical empirical educational sanity that yields the optimum dividends in teaching. To achieve this optimum is the business of wise educational administration.

What does it boil down to? To control but not to invade or unduly interfere. To watch over but not to peer or scrutinise. To advise but not to harass with counsel. To hold all strings with the necessary firmness but not to tug or slacken spasmodically. To be a living presence, to coordinate creatively, adding something to the several energies and talents of a staff—that is the business of the principal who stage-manages for good teaching, good learning. These things are not easy to achieve; they presuppose imagination, judgment, maturity. But they have existed and can be made to exist again and forever.

The most exciting part of the Sputnik story was not, at least to a non-scientist, man's triumph over outer space. It was the immediate responsiveness of American education on this planet to what had just happened off it. Wanted—in effect it said—a revolution in secondary education, because from our schools stem ultimately the material that will not only conquer outer space but will force Nature to yield up her as-yet-undiscovered secrets.

Overnight then, the curriculum and the teaching methods were overhauled, particularly in science. American education, pledged to serve the demos, began to look again at the gifted child, the superior child and to make provision for him as well as for an all-round lifting of science standards in secondary schools. In a year or so, the world of American secondary education was literate and up-to-date, scientifically speaking.

Is there any evidence that we in India are responding as America did? We, too, have had our Sputnik in the recent

Chinese invasion of India. But do we realise, as the Americans immediately did, that a revolution is needed in our secondary schools? And not in science only, but in the application of scientific method to all learning? With our usual imitativeness we have done and are doing something along the proven lines. We are investing in science teaching, in science teachers. We stress this in our speeches. We advise that. But what devastating impact do we make upon a complacent subcontinent?

The dynamic, passionate change of attitude that occurred in America has not been achieved to shake secondary school complacency out of its mediocre rut, to force it to pursue excellence, to tell it forthrightly that the old slovenly second-rateness is not good enough, and that nothing short of perfection will do if we are not to perish as an independent entity. It is not enough today to have good teachers; we need to have superlatively good teachers now and at all times.

In brass tacks what does keeping a teacher good imply? It implies a process of drastic in-service training in his subject-field, and this is particularly necessary over the middle years when men and women are apt to lose their personal skills. Teachers are kept good by a process of chiselling, and remaking that is a composite of day-to-day private study, effectively used library services, timely study leave, exchange with good teachers elsewhere in the country and with teachers from abroad.

To keep abreast of modern methods of teaching in science and language, mathematics and the social studies is the next vital thing. Every new technique must be explored and experimented with if only to test its suitability. We cannot afford to depend on dated information or dated teaching methods any more than we can afford to depend on outmoded military equipment.

It is not hard to see what is blatantly wrong with our schools today. The sustained critical habit of thought does not exist among our teachers. The object of education is to make men think clearly, think steadily, think deeply, think truly. The business of education is not to cause children to remember; it is to cause them to think for themselves. History bears out the educational judgment that those nations endure longest at a pinnacle of greatness (and not political greatness only) that have taught their people how to think, not what to think.

The why of every problem, whether in science or in the humanities, must be discovered in secondary schools if we are ever to recover from the parrot-ridden tradition that at present dominates our secondary schools.

The practising teacher's retort to all this is: "I have to get my children through the higher secondary examination. How do I do it without cramming all this information into them?"

And there is some force in the retort. For, information is at a premium in the higher secondary examination. This is so not as a corollary to, but at the expense of thinking for oneself, advancing an original view in preference to repeating a taught one, putting history to its correct use, which is to apply past experience creatively to a present predicament.

Here is an educational problem that must be faced candidly, coldly, clinically. If the examination is bad, reform or scrap it. But do not let it rob teacher and taught of what your brick-and-mortar school was raised to achieve—the pursuit of why things are as they are. There is no conflict between accurate learning and original thinking. The problem is one of stress, not of basic incompatibility. The critical habit of mind must at any cost be developed in secondary school children, now, immediately, even if this means casting overboard the long tradition of unthinking reverence that besets them in their homes, and that keeps the gods of yesterday on pedestals that should long since have been smashed.

III

Bricks and mortar attract communities of teachers and students and a good secondary school needs both good teachers and good students.

Are our students in the secondary schools, by and large, good? No, they are not. And to say this is not to denigrate or to blame them. It is merely to state a fact. I doubt if there is any system of secondary education in any progressive country of the world that produces students so unfit for employment at the terminus of secondary education and so unfit for admission to a university. Why?

I have already indicated one part of the answer. There is no alternative to good instruction in education, and good instruction is a compound of two things: first, a factual knowledge of a subject; second, a knowledge of methods of teaching that subject. We lack both in the sciences as well in the humanities.

What we lack outside this necessary field is even more serious, for we lack the ability to make responsible men and women out of intellectually promising material.

And this brings us to what is inevitable in any discussion of what bricks and mortar are required in the long run to do for human beings—the building of character.

Let me say at once that it is not, and never has been, necessary to tie up character-building and the necessary morality that underlies it with religion. Children from religious and pious homes are frequently more trivial, less truthful and less dependable than their opposites from agnostic homes in India.

Another ghost that needs to be laid at once stalks surprisingly through intellectual homes. It is that if teaching is intrinsically good, it is not necessary to think of character-building as an activity by itself. In practice, this is a wholly fallacious view. Children outstandingly good at mathematics, who have had the good fortune to get good teaching and the good sense to respond to it, are often dishonest, given to subterfuge and intrigue and are deeply impregnated with inherited prejudice which is the negation of mental and moral clarity.

One of the most entertainingly profitable occupations for anyone anxious to analyse what is wrong with our secondary schools today in terms of character-building is to glance at the stream of fiction that has been, and is being, produced in the United Kingdom for adolescent girls. The British have produced from a variety of sources, some public, some private, novels for girls in which there appears to be tacit agreement on the essentials of character for their society. Angela Brazil, Dorita Fairlie Bruce, Sheila Stuart, Monica Marsden, Margaret Biggs and even Enid Blyton imply in their books a code of thought and behaviour that Britain expects of her schoolgirls. They must be kind and learn to live together. They must be honourable and, in matters affecting personal and public integrity, above reproach. They must be loyal to people and to institutions. They must develop proportion with a balance between true seriousness and necessary fun and laughter. The nicest girls in these books of high morality are surprisingly not stodgy or repellantly moral; they are attractive, helpful, competent and collectively aware of their neighbours.

What have we in India done to produce a comparable stream of fiction that portrays living to fit our needs in 1964? Nothing, for if we had done something in the sixteen years of our educational independence we would by now have something to offer our children that is based in India and springs naturally out of it.

What code should be inculcated into Indian schoolgirls today? A code written or unwritten (that is, implied) on these lines:

First, the need to speak and act the truth under all circumstances without reservation, without compromise, without subtlety and without distinction.

Second, the need to develop a sense of responsibility for oneself and the community one lives in, the quality of dependability, the capacity to recognise and to honour a commitment.

Third, the need to develop conscious leadership with a sense of humour to offset and destroy self-importance. This leadership must be based on courage, fearlessness and dependability.

Unless we can adopt such a code and make it, through literature, second nature to our children, cultivating it in the formative years that are spent in secondary schools, we will not have the kind of nation that takes crises in its stride. Pride in one's country is not automatic. All praise, all love, it seems, needs human meriting. Patriotism, which is pride in all that lies behind the life of a people as also what lies within it, cannot be achieved permanently on a high emotional plane unless it is rooted in the strong habits and convictions of everyday living. And everyday living grows out of everyday schooling.

If I have particularly stressed a code for girls, it is for two reasons. First, I know more about girls and their upbringing than I do about boys, and have read more literature about girls than about boys. But there is a better second reason for the point that I make. Unless we take the business of girls' and women's education more seriously than we have done in the past, we run the risk of educating individuals but not families or a nation. Sheer economic necessity must now drive us into educating girls with a compulsive urgency that will take no refusal. For, women have an extraordinary way at all ages of setting implicit standards in and for society. Frivolous women make frivolous societies. Educated women make educated societies.

This, then, is the final moral of the bricks and mortar that the Socialist character in Winifred Holtby's *South Riding* advocated. With him, I believe in bricks and mortar because bricks and mortar give education a local habitation and a name without which the solid, substantial benefits of teaching, of corporate learning and character-building cannot be achieved.

I believe in bricks and mortar because they attract good communities of good teachers and good students, and all good education is a compound of good teachers and good students. We need to insist on perfectionism in teaching, nothing less will do for the times.

And with this backdrop of bricks and mortar, with the compelling drive of superlatively good teaching and a code, such as I have described, of conduct for children, we shall have the best students in the world. Then, and then only, will patriotism become what it should be, not an emotional, irrational and isolated impulse, but a daily, silent, corporate quality of service without vanity, as silent, corporate and serviceable as the bricks and mortar that symbolise the abiding triumph of man over the dark hosts of ignorance.

2

Teach English: What and How?

I

Ten years ago this article and its sequel would have been unnecessary. We had not then lost the sound of English as a living language. We were not in danger of losing the use of English as a language of intellection. Today, for those who regard English as more than a mime for communication, India is in extremis. Every educationist who holds that English is relevant for any stage or part of education must be willing to think this problem out for himself. We are concerned less with the specialist whose business is English literature as a postgraduate field of specialisation than with the generalist who seeks to use English in India in order to keep learning alive, up-to-date and excellent in the sciences and the humanities.

An instrument is neither good nor bad; it is neutral. It can be studied with the cold, clinical eye of expediency. It need not and should not breed partisanship. Nothing is here for passion, nothing for pride or prejudice. Anger is irrelevant; so is that muted affection with which aristocratic old ladies (and some gentlemen, too) regard the language of sophistication. We are examining English as an instrument whereby the Indian student of 1964 can think freely and boldly, analytically and constructively, can reach an outer world of progress and can proclaim attitudes, habits, views that may be distinctively Indian.

There are probably few in India today who argue that English should be banished altogether from the curriculum of secondary schools and universities. The argument is one of accent and place. Accord English a secondary place, so the argument runs, since it is not native to the mass of the inhabitants of India and because, therefore, it must handicap original and profound thought. But, say these people, whether out of conviction or as a concession to our increasingly liberal times, standards of English must be maintained. Those who urge this argument are concerned hardly at all with spoken English. This, they maintain, generally implicitly (explicitly if pressed), is a frill in a country that cannot afford to be purist in language. We do not want our students today to speak with an "Oxford accent," they say (as if our students ever did), but they must be able to use English lucidly to express their meaning clearly and fully.

Every educational decision today is dictated by the consideration of whether this or that activity will be marketable. English will be acquired with competence only if to do so raises marketability. If English continues to pay in strictly economic terms it will continue to be acquired, assuming always that the conditions for acquiring it exist in the country. If it does not pay in strictly economic terms to acquire English with proficiency, it will not be studied with any earnestness. For perfectionism, that urge for craftsmanship that is independent of economic reward, is not an academic ailment that afflicts us in our subcontinent.

Advocates for relegating English to a subsidiary place in secondary and university education have never squarely faced what they intend to do to ensure the availability of competent teachers (by world standards) at either level. Result: the gap that constantly exists in India between educational aspiration and fact, educational theory and practice. It is more consistent to banish English altogether from our curriculum, than to seek "to maintain standards" without spelling out a practical programme that will ensure the availability of competent teachers of English on a scale on which this subcontinent requires those teachers.

What English shall we teach our children, rural and urban, at secondary and at university level? On this question hangs another: what is the choice before India in 1964?

It must be clear to anyone who has studied a language with any seriousness that a language can be acquired proficiently only when it is constantly heard. That is why it is an integral part of any higher language course in a progressive country for the student to spend part of his course, perhaps his long vacations, in the country whose language he is studying. At some stage it will be necessary for him to dream in that language, and unless he constantly hears a language, he will not dream in it.

We in India today do not generally hear English spoken except derivatively. We do not hear it constantly; we do not hear it frequently. There are some areas in which we do not hear it at all. Very rarely, if at all, do we hear it spoken perfectly. Students in rural areas, under the impression that they have spoken English for some years, arrive at Delhi to take a scholarship interview, are confronted with a real live Englishman speaking living English, can scarcely decipher what he says and do worse than they need. He, for his part, must revise the notion, rashly conceived, that his mother tongue is still current in India. If the rural Indian student has heard English it is through broadcasts or a tape-recording. In the normal course, he has met no Englishman; most of his fellow countrymen do not speak English to him, and when they do, are not particular about enunciation, rhythm, pronunciation or pitch.

There was a time when Indians learnt their English from Englishmen in India, and being facile of ear and mind, learnt to speak good English. This period was succeeded by one in which Indians learnt to speak English from Indians who had learnt from Englishmen. Not so good, but not so bad either. Finally, today, Indians learn English from Indians who have learnt it from Indians. There is no danger of their speaking it with the much-maligned "Oxford accent." They speak it with an intonation so heavily transferred from their mother tongue, that it is not a language that can honourably be described as English at all. Just such a person is the average teacher of English in Indian secondary schools. If he is in a city, he does not make so bad a job of teaching the language because he hears it still reasonably well spoken. If he is in a rural area, he is often at sea. What passes for English among students of some of our rural institutes (which are postsecondary institutions) is a language that eludes categorisation. Yet the rural institutes are unwilling to give up the study of Shakespeare and English poetry.

Can we shut both eye and ear to this lack of good spoken English? Can we argue, as do the exponents of the English-as-a-foreign-language view, that it does not much matter what English in India sounds like, provided the student has a knowledge of it adequate to the business of reading books in it and understanding them?

To accept such a view is merely to promote decline. For, consider: somewhere, the ordinary student of English at secondary and university level is going to run into an English poem. Perhaps only a narrative poem, but still a poem. All poetry is written for the ear, not for the eye. Much of the "meaning" of poetry is transmitted to the mind and the sensibilities through the ear. Pronounce it wrongly, offend against its rhyme and rhythm and assonance, and you have effectively destroyed what it is saying.

But, bother poetry, they say. Life in India of 1964 is prose, economic prose. Let our students read Alfred Marshall, let them read Lord Acton and even Edmund Burke without too much fuss about rhythm, etc. Let them. The content of all these may be understood without good spoken English, but they can be understood very much better with well-spoken English. For such proverbs as "the magic of property turns sand to gold," "magnanimity in politics is not seldom the truest wisdom and great empires and little minds go ill together," and "power corrupts, absolute power corrupts absolutely," are much more pregnant with meaning to someone who has grown to speak instinctive easy English than it is to a student, feeling his way from his mother tongue to English in a kind of blind fumble for unfamiliar meanings. Only complete ease in a spoken language confers complete ease in a written language. Compromise on the spoken word and you intensify the rate and depth of decline in English.

What English should we teach our children in secondary schools in the big cities of India? On the same principle that an illiterate adult cannot and should not be made to acquire literacy through concepts so elementary that by their lack of interest they retard progress, so secondary school children in India, starting English for the first time at a comparatively late stage, should not be fed on "The-Cat-Is-On-The-Mat" sentences. Nor should texts prescribed for the Higher Secondary examination consist, as they do at present in Delhi, of Will and Charlie Mayo, an elementary booklet that is an affront to intelligent children of sixteen about to enter a university. English texts must be at par in concept and statement with general intellectual maturity. Also prescribed for the Delhi higher secondary schools is an admirable text, The Story of Man, that, though simple in statement, is on a subject sufficiently advanced to engage the attention of children in the growing years. Abridged editions of Dickens and Jane Austen still leave something to be desired by oversimplifying the original and writing down to children. We may err seriously and permanently by not exacting enough of our children.

There is a real danger today that the average secondary school child, linguistically an extremely low average, will set the standard for all children in this age group. There are, however, children at Indian secondary schools today (and they come chiefly from the upper middle classes of the country), 'who are quite equal to difficult English texts, prose and poetry, and who need not be depressed by the lowest common denominator that presides over our schools. The answer to this problem, if we are in earnest about raising English standards, is to have, in addition to the three set papers in English, an advanced language (English) paper at higher secondary level and to reward proficiency in it. English classics in the original—Jane Austen, Scott, Dickens, Thackeray, the Bronte sisters, Mrs Gaskell. "George Eliot, Hardy and well-considered and chosen classics and semi-classics from the later 20th century—could all be included in such a curriculum. If educational planning must plan for numbers, it must also make provision somewhere for the pursuit of excellence. It is the out-of-the-way child, not the common-or-garden one (for whom it seems today all plans are tailored), who will lift us out of our educational rut and show us the merits of excellence over quantity. The withdrawn child at a secondary school, who has not found his level because his needs have not been spelt out or seen to be of abiding educational importance (though they may confer no obvious economic benefit), is the child who must be catered for if this country is to prosper. Yet for this withdrawn and sometimes patently superior child, we do nothing today.

Shakespeare has been banished from the higher secondary, largely, it would appear, as a counsel of despair, though he is still present in the Indian School Certificate, for which we must be grateful. Here again, an advanced paper at secondary level might well take in Shakespearean Comedy, *Twelfth Night, The Merchant of Venice, As You Like It,* and more than comedy, *The Tempest*. It would be a truly sad commentary on our English teaching if our children had to make Shakespeare's acquaintance through current Hindi translations of *Macbeth* and *Othello*.

One of the dangers of having no well-formulated' programme to secure competence in English at university level is that one constantly slurs over the difference between English as a language of communication and English as a language of intellection. "It is raining now but it will soon be fine," is an example of a statement of communication. It does not call for an understanding of any involved concept of living or being or doing. It is not difficult to achieve this level of English though such a level implies a knowledge of idiomatic English. Compare with this a statement such as "ripeness is all," or "the child is father of the man," or "human praise needs human meriting," or "the long day's task is done and we must sleep," or "if winter comes can spring be far behind?" to observe that a whole circle of ideas, some intellectual, some sensuous-cum intellectual, is implied and must be grasped and accepted before the meaning of the new phrase is perceived. Understanding implies the steady use of a language recollected in tranquillity.

The development of a language of intellection implies a passage of rime. Only time and the stretch of sound over time with all that includes in the texture of thinking and feeling, can make minds ready to use a language for intellectual purposes.

It will be argued, and has been argued, that English has no monopoly in the capacity to express profundities of intellect or sensibility, and that other channels have been and must now be found. But surely no nation gives up what it has known to confer power. Our hold over English as a language of intellection/ abandoned in this generation, will be lost forever, for there is no recovering, in the absence of constantly spoken English, what it has taken over a hundred years to acquire with British association. And losing it, we lose that easy access to the world's heritage of intellectual writing in the English language that will tend not to get smaller and smaller as we abandon English, but inevitably larger as English becomes the thinking language of Africa, Sri Lanka and the

West Indies and continues to be the spoken, and thinking language of, in addition to Great Britain, America, Australia, Canada, and New Zealand.

II

Assuming that India wishes her students at secondary and university level to be taught English as both a language of communication and a language of intellection, how shall we go about this crucial problem in 1964?

No programme has yet been formulated on a national basis (though Kerala has done something regionally) to achieve excellence in either of these directions. There are institutes for teaching English at various places, south and north, but their capacity to train teachers of English is pathetically small relative to our demand for them. Also, institutes such as those set up do not guarantee to the practising teacher in India the continuous sound of English as a living language that is necessary to the sustained rnastery of this swiftly changing and growing language.

In the first place, we must accept the datum that languages must be taught with the same emphasis on accuracy, excellence, lightness with which we teach mathematics. We do not easily acquiesce in incorrect formulae; why, then, should we easily acquiesce in incorrect phrase, pronunciation, idiom, grammar, spelling? We are almost deliberately casual and slovenly in the teaching and learning of language, most especially today English, and we take refuge, or the less moral of us do, in its being a "foreign language" that was overrated in the wicked past, and that deserves to suffer now in the inevitably swing of a historic pendulum. Unless, however, we are determined to seek nothing less than perfection in English teaching and learning we shall never be even moderately good. This is the first requisite, as a goal^ perfection; as a condition of teaching and learning English, accuracy.

Next, we can no more gloss over spoken English than in teaching music, we can gloss over phrasing. Sound is vital to all language. One does not know a language till one has learnt to speak it with fluency, ease, delight, mastery. Nothing less than this will do. Only when a language is acquired to perfection for speaking purposes^ will it be acquired without resistance and with delight for reading and writing purposes. There is no clear educational line of demarcation between the spoken and the written word, and those who seek to draw this imaginary line today are doing education in India a lasting disservice.

How shall we secure excellence in spoken English in India today? Very simply, by using the neglected ear. By speaking to the ear. By making students at all levels listen for days, weeks, months before they begin to speak, read, learn, write. Till they have listened long enough to dream in English, they are not ready to speak it. Quite suddenly, good teachers of English will find their pupils wake upto the beauty and richness of the language. Use tape-recordings where live human voices are not available. Let the children hear excellent, good and indifferent English, registering by ear the difference between them. Let them instinctively grasp through the ear the essential difference between English and non-English.

A slow, repetitive process, but it yields increasing dividends. Every teacher of English must have a sharp ear. Every teacher of English must have a trained ear. Every teacher of English must be made to pass a difficult viva in English before he/she is permitted to teach English in our secondary schools. Once there, constant in-service refresher courses in spoken and written English will keep people up to scratch. Where possible, and in association with such bodies as the British Council, teachers must go abroad to England on three-month courses to study methods of teaching English. They should also be encouraged to write to educational journals and to daily newspapers to relate experiences in this kind. Our teachers are often bad writers because they are unpractised writers. There is nothing like the written word to destroy that chief pedagogical defect of pomposity.

What is vital in all this is that the teacher shall grasp and continuously be conscious of the difference between a living, growing, dynamic language and a dead, literary language. The language that the teacher inherited from Dickens, Scott, Hardy via an Indian university, may bring him private delight, but is strictly a dead language. The idiom of languages changes. This is true of English, that has become the spoken property of America, Australia, Canada, and New Zealand and the thinking property of Sri Lanka, the West Indies, and Africa, than it is of other languages with a more restricted area of usage. The English language has changed noticeably in the last two decades. Much that was written in the 1940s is now out of date. How much truer then that what was written in the nineteenth century and the early years of the twentieth century is dead! Only going abroad, listening to the growing English speak their changing language, will make the teacher of English in Indian schools and colleges understand the difference between English yesterday, today and tomorrow.

All teachers of English should be required to belong to up-to-date libraries and should be able to certify regular reading in modem English literature. Fortunately our big cities today are reasonably well-equipped with such libraries, and fees are sufficiently low to be an invitation to the teaching world to use books.

It is probably asking for the moon to insist today that teachers shall be sensitive to the element of beauty in English writing that, for want of a better word. I will call "style." There was a time in my early teaching years when we could hope to have the experience that I had with a girl of fourteen writing on "Castles in the Air." She concluded her essay thus: "Man is a dreamer and builds as he dreams. He will go on dreaming and building till he reaches in the Golden City the temple not made with hands. Then, perhaps, he will stop dreaming, stop building, because it will no longer be necessary to do either."

It was worth teaching English for drear}" years to have one such essay. It meant that someone, somewhere, understood that language exists for more than "communication."

At university level the chief danger to the acquisition of perfect English as a language of intellection is the attitude that we can no longer be purist. This is a variation on the "we-do-not-need-to-have-an-Oxford-accent" theme. Once this attitude creeps in, in a country such as ours that is all too willing to be satisfied with half-and-half quality, it tends to dominate education and dictate its contours. Every teacher of English must make it clear that there is no slip however small that will not be corrected in speech, reading, and writing. Teachers of English at university level must be as exacting as their opposites at secondary level; indeed more so, for they have the added responsibility of pressing English to its logical extreme as a language of intellection.

It is not possible to cultivate English as a language of intellection in people who dislike it, resist it and learn it for economic reasons only. Therefore, students studying in English, and studying English must, by the time they come up to a university, have been converted to the beauty, richness and power of the language. Failing this, all university life becomes strife and bargaining between teacher and taught, and the life of a university tutor is fraught with the bitterness and frustration of non-achievement.

Much more life must now be infused into the teaching of English at university level. Even those who do not read, English as a special subject at postgraduate level (for preference here argues a joy in the subject that ensures hard work) must be made to see for themselves the joy of handling English to perfection. More time needs to be given to speaking this language in debate and drama, seminar and tutorial. More time needs to be spent encouraging the perfect writing of English. Newspapers do the student and teaching community a real service by inviting students to contribute to their columns. Nationwide competitions reflecting the way of life we prize in

1964 must be encouraged. The world is anxious to know how we live and think, and who but our young at universities-today can tell the world genuinely and without boastfulness how we go about the common task? But it is essential that those who write should write unfractured, competent, excellent English. Unless trained early to write this English, what they have to say may never reach that outer world that is straining to know the Indian people's hopes and fears, their dreams and disenchantments.

We have gone all out, and rightly, to expand and reform our facilities for science and technology teaching and learning. In doing so, we tend to overlook the need for perfection in other fields, and more particularly in language. The language most neglected today is English. There is no national plan for its improvement; of the maintenance of standards it is almost ironic to speak. Unless this plan is formulated here and now, we go in danger of suffering that isolation of half-understood and badly-expressed English that will work to our international detriment in the demanding world of 1964.

3

Teaching History in Indian Schools

It is customary at intervals for someone to raise the cry of an institution or a creed in danger. So often has this been done in the past so superfluously that public scepticism is not unjustified. The cry of a subject-field in danger is quite another matter. Those who have eyes to see, ears to hear, have only to consider how history is taught at Indian schools today to realise that something is sufficiently wrong to justify alarm. I would not suggest that this is peculiar to history. Nevertheless, history is a field that has suffered so badly by neglect and misguided judgment that it may be profitable to single it out for discussion.

India has had in recent years to concentrate on the teaching of science and technology. No one disputes the need for this bias at a time when the world stands on the edge of a scientific revolution and we, like the rest of the world, have passed into the age of the sputnik. Nevertheless, there is a danger that we will pass unsuspectingly into the age of technology only to find in ten years that we are without top-ranking or even good historians.

The prospect of such a future automatically depresses the present and the teacher of history in our schools is already the frustrated creature that the handmaiden of an outworn creed is apt to become. The secondary schools of India are today teaching a curriculum in history that is in drastic need of revision, and they are teaching that curriculum by methods so dated that we would appear to have passed through the last twenty-five years of educational experiment in this subject without impression. We are still teaching British History and to this there can be no objection except that the History of Europe is not less important than that of Britain, and the History of the Middle East and South-East Asia is, from some points of view, more, important. Nevertheless, we are teaching British History and a period of British History—the Stuarts—that many of us would regard as being more absorbing, dazzling and romantic than any other in the story of Britain.

But how is this history being taught to children with insufficient background in the history of Britain, who have never seen her and are, for the most part, never likely to see her? From bad and badly printed textbooks that reiterate the hard and sometimes dull fact, but do nothing to portray that memorable struggle for sovereignty in terms of personality or idea, that do not attempt to relate history in Britain to history in India or other parts of the world. No effort is made to open the doors of historical fiction—and this abounds in the Stuart period—to Indian children. No attempt is made to dramatize the era of Charles I or of that other "Good King Charles" whose intellect and charm have survived for millions outside Britain, or that tapestry of highly controversial, highly partisan life of kingly passions, prejudices, conflicts that is of the stuff of drama. The entire procession of history passes into a bad textbook, eras strung together with dates held problematically by a streamer "dateline." For apparently the "date-line" is the latest arrival in technique. (It is a long streamer of pointless paper on which a child laboriously grafts date after date in the attempt to provide history with its scaffolding.)

What a Way to Teach History!

And when the damage I have described has been done,

we go on to worse. We are provided with an examination under a higher secondary board that disposes of the Stuart period and, perhaps, also the preceding Tudor period, in a series of factual questions that any child in the Fifth Class of an English-medium school in India could answer perfectly without knowing the ABC of history.

Let it be said that the crime is committed with sweeping consistency. It starts without inspiration in a bad textbook; it continues without inspiration through a teacher who crams the merciless facts of the period into young children; it ends without inspiration in the dry-as-dust examination paper that demands its pound of flesh on the facts that the uninspired and uninspiring teacher has crammed into bored children insisting, for better measure, that the children shall inscribe and immortalise them on a date-line.

We are teaching Indian History with a panoramic sweep that suggests that our children can digest history with greater ease and speed than any other children in the world. Nevertheless, and even if we overlook the vast sweep of the curriculum, how are we teaching Indian History? "Facts," said Mr. Gradgrind, "facts, facts, facts." I have watched the performance of history teachers at some of the country's higher secondary schools. I have studied the examination papers given to children at higher secondary level. If both were calculated to alienate the children from a love of their past and to discourage the discovery of the future in the past, they could hardly have done better. The Guptas, the Mughals, the Afghans and the Marathas are all alike consigned to that museum of the past in which what was, and is most living in the ideas of men, remains most dead for their children. No comparisons are instituted, no study made of the brevity of empires, of their sustained and common tendencies to fall apart, of the difficulties of delegating power and the constant problems in governing a subcontinent of India's size and complexity, that persist down to our own times.

This is a plea for a change of curriculum in history as it is for a revolution in methods of teaching it. For, if the only way that we can teach the Stuart period is the way that I have described, it would be better not to teach it at all.

The textbook has always been, will always be, an instrument of subsidiary importance in the business of teaching. The first, natural and necessary agent is the teacher. But the teacher of history in India, confronted with the steep decline in the utility, popularity and respect for his subject, regards himself as a second-grade citizen whose contribution to the national store of learning is doomed and is, in any case, of purely theoretic value. He does not realise that to teach history carelessly, lazily, and as if it does not really matter because it is not readily marketable, is to be guilty of an educational crime. For it is to rob education of that intellectual passion without which it is meaningless and had much better not be imparted.

The first essential in teaching children history is to go back to the roots of history and there is no root more penetrating than the geography of the country. Let us, therefore, turn to the immediate geography of India.

Empty the classroom and turn the children into the open. At every suitable season, in every year, turn them out of the red-brick buildings that we call schools, away from the date-line, the textbook, the blackboard, the drone of uninspired teaching, but do not turn them upon national monuments or museums yet, for even this is a second-rate way of teaching history. The monument is a historical result; it is not a cause of history. The museum is an assemblage of things that does not necessarily reflect the thinking of an age, unless these things are superlatively well-organised, and our museums are not yet superlatively well-organised.

If we are to revolutionise the teaching of history in our schools, it must be through sheer joy, for only a movement of joy in education will now lead our children to re-discover their country. And was there ever a country like India for diversity and range and wonder at the cruelty, compassion and inclusiveness of Nature, and Man! From Mysore, luxuriant, sandal-sweet-smelling as the winds blow, across her lakes and wooded hills, to the Punjab, lively, hard, resistant, unyielding; from Kerala, lagoon-studded, to Odisha, with its gleaming sea and long surf-ridden coasts; from the springing rice-fields of Assam to the red-earthed Deccan; from Kashmir and Kulu to the Western Ghats, rich in history and rugged in natural beauty, no citizen of any country could ask for a chart or map or a spectacle of geography or history more varied, eloquent and revealing.

The Youth Hostel Movement, that has started in India but has as yet made little headway, can use the clarion cry of "Discover India" to stimulate this process. We need maps; we need hostels; but above all, we need information. All this and more the Youth Hostel Movement can supply. In this task, it needs to be supported by educational institutions, by schools, colleges and universities that must organise regular visits to historical sites and that must, in a drive to teach, take children over the length and breadth of this subcontinent to force it to yield its historical secrets. What it looks like, what it is like, what it yields, all this the child who travels through India will learn to know. Automatically, the basic lesson of history is taught and learnt. The history of Delhi, the history of Maharashtra are what they are because these parts of the country needed men of steel and men of intrepidity to conquer and rule them.

Once open up the countryside and the rest will be the story of discovery that is the reward of good teachers. Of his own initiative, the child will open the creaking doors of the school library; he will look at maps and records. He will read historic fiction that will round off the story of his land.

Nor is that all. Dramatise history as a regular part of teaching. Instead of the pathetic school drama that is served up regularly to admiring, condoning parents, teach both children and parents history through regular school-day drama. Commission one-act plays on Indian History. Produce one-act plays and teach the children to produce them. This will drive them into the study of art and costume history, and the doors of the past will swing slowly open through the irresistible media of clothes, customs, manners and idiom.

Not long ago, St. Thomas' Higher Secondary School, New Delhi, produced a panoramic pageant of ballet, music and drama to tell the story of the Gandhian era. It was the best history lesson that I have ever had, and the fact that I was no longer a child, did not debar me from the delight of learning what had never been taught so well before. Inspiration, collective work, the assemblage with joy of one thousand children made this a superb spectacle, as entertainment as well as a good history lesson. Entertainment, however, was only a first step. The idea followed. Like the proverbial seed it grew. Discussion was conducted in the classroom; and the children learnt that Gandhian history provided them with those targets for today, the historic point of which they had so consistently missed earlier. They began to understand the authentic business of history.

It is the business of history to make us not comfortable but uncomfortable. It is its business to destroy complacency, to stimulate discontent, to draw the human soul into uneasy life when it is in danger of achieving easy death. And it is its business somewhere to restore to the spirit of man that symbol of a soaring destiny that fired the Elizabethans, and that led Columbus through mutiny and peril to a new world that he fell upon and kissed with the passion in discovery, with which our children, too, will speak, when they discover what has always been, but has not always been known to be.

4
Looking for Leadership

We use the word "leadership" today as once, not long ago, we used the word "Mesopotamia." No one is very clear about what it means; nevertheless, everyone seems to suffer from the ambition to qualify for it. When I meet assemblages of young men, chiefly undergraduates, I am aware that I have only to talk about leadership to rivet their straying attention upon me. The word has achieved mystic, as well as psychological, properties. Everyone is looking for a leader. Everyone is hopeful that he will be identified from among thousands of "followers" as a leader.

Now all this seems very strange to me. For, "Leader" acquired over the late 1930s and 40s of this century the flavour of dictatorship that several millions of people the world over fought to destroy. Having destroyed dictatorship's more articulate embodiments, we then, so it seems, settled down to accept the fact that without leaders we are lost and that, for every thousand or ten thousand sheep, there must be a shepherd. Either we were wrong in the first place to fight "Fuehrers," or else it must be that within a democracy we mean something very different from what totalitarian peoples mean when they use this cunning word.

It is as much a legacy of wars to destroy leadership of the dictatorial kind as of the two hundred years of subjection in which Indians were either denied responsibility or were unable to grasp it, that we now equate the leader with a political leader. That is not unnatural, but it is wrong and dangerous and wasteful. It is not unnatural, because power is most easy to symbolise and most essential to seize and hold in the sphere of politics. It is wrong, dangerous and wasteful to identify leadership with political leadership, because there are in a democracy as many kinds and degrees of leadership as there are, or should be, kinds of activity and degrees of authority. It seems to me that today our need of leadership in schools and colleges, in town councils and village panchayats, in official and non-official committees, in administration and commerce, in medicine and engineering, in writing and painting and the theatre—in a word, in the seemingly unlimited activities that make life in a democracy worth living—is much more necessary of cultivation than leadership in the parliaments of man. This political leadership that all men and some women appear to cherish is probably indispensable to the governance of the human race. But at every stage in its growth it presupposes and leans upon the many-sided leadership in everyday life that I have referred to. Indeed, without this substratum of personal, academic, scientific, social, artistic, and practical day-to-day leadership, there could be no leadership of the kind that the democracy par excellence demands of its political workers.

What do we ask for in our leaders today? In India the leader has not always been a man of shining intellect or sensational brilliance. Such men do appear. In their presence, history is made. Their phrases pass into the proverbs of mankind. But, by and large, the contribution of these men to the growth of a democracy is comparatively small. There is no evidence that the Buddha was a great intellect, and the chances are that Gandhi would have repudiated, with the final simplicity that characterised his search for Truth, the attribute of "brilliance."

The leader we ask for in the fields in which we need him most must have some inescapable element of greatness, but he need not be a legend of intellect, intuitive or logical. He must have integrity or, since it is a word more easily grasped, though less easily defined, "character."

There is always some danger that a people to whom the mind means as much as it does to us in India may indiscriminately exploit every faculty of the mind without weighing the wisdom of this piece of mental sleight-of-hand. For, consider—the human mind is as prone to cunning as to the wise subtlety which Christ advocated when he said: "Be ye as simple as a dove and as cunning as a serpent." It is as prone to intrigue as to mathematical analysis, to inertia as to the tranquil reflection that is necessary to the growth of intellect. Ultimately, what decides us to accept one facet of mind and to reject another so closely linked with it that the one may be described as a virtue of a defect, the other as a defect of a virtue? As I see it, "character." Only character can consciously determine for us how our various faculties are developed, to what degree they are developed, to what end they are developed. Only character can supply the plan and the proportion that make the cultivation of the human mind the supreme achievement and the most ambitious target of all man's reckoning.

Nor is this character, without which leadership cannot exist, a product of pure intellect. It is the composite of early conditioning so mechanical that the child adopts it as it adopts meal-time; of feeling tempered by experience; of logical deduction from experience; and ultimately, of a fearlessness that, ingrained at first by wise conditioning, is later formed by circumstances and is finally confirmed by the situations and roles that a seemingly capricious fate allots all of us throughout our lives.

To make character the end of both education and living is, I should say, the function of our schools and colleges, of our teachers, and of those who today dominate the many-sided life of our cities and villages. Our best reason for remembering the prophets is not that they told us what we did not know before, but that they acted as we did not dare to act till we saw in them just this character that made us, in the moment of perception, greater than we knew.

5

Freedom and Authority

The history of mankind is punctuated with movements in favour of either authority or freedom. As one advances, the other recedes. It is superfluous, and outside the scope of this article, to analyse, the reasons for which authority dominates the minds of men in one era and retires in another before the advancing forces of liberation. Enough to say that pressed too far, authority inevitably stimulates a hunger for freedom in every direction—political, social, educational. Disorder and violence bring authority into being; stagnation stimulates the urge for growth and freedom. Apparently, human life is a composite of movements towards authority and against it; towards freedom and against it. Where then do the two meet?

Educationally, it is not sensible to take sides for or against authority, for or against freedom. The need for growth is evident at every stage of education—primary, secondary, higher. With maturity comes a demand for freedom that no wise educationist can resist. The question for us to consider, however, is not the stage at which freedom should be associated with authority (for it should be associated with authority at every stage), but the ways in which authority and freedom should abide together so that the product of their combined impact will be a mature creature.

Be it said at once that both authority and freedom are means to an end and that end, the full development of the human personality within the geographic, social and cultural limits of a community. We may interpret the community in world or national dimensions. We may interpret it in terms of the family or society, but the individual must be adjusted to his environment and to the extent that it is so, he must acknowledge authority outside himself as well as within himself, acknowledge the urge for freedom within himself and the urge for freedom in the society to which he belongs. More practically, the problem of where authority begins and ends, and where freedom ends and begins are concrete problems of discipline.

It is a truism to say that the only desirable discipline is self-discipline. Self-discipline is not easy to achieve, and if we ask children in elementary and secondary schools to achieve this either quickly or at all, we are asking for the proverbial moon. The only discipline that comes naturally to children in groups is a discipline exercised by that group. Rounding-off angularities, smoothing rough edges are all part of the business of being at school. This is the kind of incidental discipline that is good for all children and that no child ultimately regrets having had. There is, in addition, the inevitable discipline of a time-table and a curriculum, the discipline implicit in the presence of teachers and a headmistress. Disciplines from the home may complement or conflict with the discipline of the school. Ordinarily, parental discipline should enhance the discipline of the school and be enhanced by it.

If, today, we in India consider the question of discipline with new eyes, it is because we see that the child in the elementary and the secondary school needs for its development a larger measure of freedom than it has had in the past. Conversely, it needs a different kind of authority than it has had in the past.

Time was when the Indian child accepted parental or school order without much question. To obey was automatic. This is no longer so. The questioning spirit that began elsewhere has permeated this country, and the waves of student indiscipline at universities have touched the upper levels of secondary schools. The child will no longer easily acquiesce in authority at secondary level. She will question, argue and defend herself. It is for educational authority to be, not above reproach (for then it would be infallible and superhuman) but to be able to bear scrutiny, to render unto the child what the child has a right to ask of it in terms of ability, integrity, dignity and maturity. It is hard, paying teachers what we do, treating teachers as we do, to expect these qualities of them. Yet nothing less will support them within the school. Freedom has come to stay in so far as the child is concerned. Her right to question can no longer be disputed. It is, therefore, the business of the teacher and of educational authority to meet children half-way.

From the standpoint of the child's freedom, it is clearly important for parents to think harder than they have done in the past. The adolescent can no longer be treated as an automaton who grows automatically upwards from childhood to maturity, without problems, maladjustments and those unanswerable questions that parents and teachers have to cope with. Adolescence must be recognised as a difficult period in which an essentially good and kind child, who will eventually achieve maturity and wisdom, passes through a period of adjustment, unhappiness, superstition, weariness, fatigue, discontent, frustration and irritation with the world at large. These irritations are particularly focussed on parents and teachers, and if parents and teachers cannot survive this period of questioning, scrutiny, criticism, they are obviously not worth the high prestige that they have inherited from a dead past and the reverence in which they hope to be held in a beckoning future

The Indian child of 1964, whether at elementary or at secondary level, is apt to ask questions that were not asked before. These questions will have to be answered. She will express opinions with a positiveness that may shock parents and teachers, but that will have to be accepted as part of an opinionated development. The secondary school child will do more than express opinions; she will seek often to tear down authority and use such institutions as seminars, discussion groups and school parliaments to bring authority under scrutiny and perhaps even into disrepute. If authority is strong, it need have no fear of this criticism, this potential opposition. For in the long run children are as sensible as an adult electorate. They may think and talk nonsense, but they make the right active decisions. And respect for authority will not waver or fail if authority in the long run conducts itself with the stability, wisdom and good sense that automatically destroy potential and inexperienced opposition. One reason why a child without authority is a bored child is that children desire, up to a certain point, to be told what to do. They wish to feel the presence of authority even where they resent the detail of authoritative command.

It is as well today for all parents and all teachers in India to remember the men and women in the world's history who have spoken with authority. There was one who struck men as different "from the Scribes and Pharisees" and whom "the waves and winds obeyed" because he spoke "as one having authority." Socrates, whose name dominates the world of truth and education after twenty centuries, was a man who questioned authority with freedom and freedom with authority. This man, cheerfully drinking his cup of hemlock (having spoken to his judges in the immortal words: "Therefore, ye judges, be of good cheer and know that to a good man no evil thing can happen") symbolises the perfect compromise between the freedom to think, ask and question, and the authority that knows that anarchy and disorder are bad for the human spirit.

"Whither freedom and authority in India? To, I hope, that Socratic compromise in which authority will see that to justify itself, it has to be better than that which it rules; and freedom will see that its only rational meaning is the right to determine its own restraints with wisdom alike for personal growth and collective strength.

6
The Translation of Plays

It is generally assumed by those with a mission to make the world one in drama as in everything else that the "open sesame" to the world's cultural riches and heritage, no matter how varied these may be, lies in the will to make the local universal. But if it had been as easy as that, it would not have taken two wars of worldwide dimension to show that mankind is by inheritance more apart than united.

Drama presents that special field in the Fine Arts that is at once uniting and divisive. It is uniting because it appeals to all universal love of action. It moves and has its being in movement. On the other hand, to the extent that it uses language as its medium of movement, it divides, for nothing so portrays and symbolises a way of life, and differing ways of life, as language.

I have heard it said by experts in drama that classic drama is the property of the world. That is true in just about the same sense as that other "truism" that all the religions of man teach the same truth or truths. In fact, Moliere's plays are no more the property of India, though they have been translated into Indian languages, than Shakespeare is the property of Uttar Pradesh or Madhya Pradesh or Bihar because Macbeth has been played in Hindi. There are plays in French, notably the work of Sartre, that have certain qualities that transcend local and geographical limits and that are manifestly plays of idea that override peculiarities inherent in a particular way of life. Plays about life and death, crime and punishment, love and hatred, in a word, the eternal human passions, are better subjects for translation than comedies of manners such as *The Importance of Being Earnest* or *Le Bourgeois Gentilhomme*; but even these plays partake of their country of origin—its thought, attitudes, wit, and language of approvals and disapprovals. *The Clay Cart* has been rendered in several languages of the world as has Shakuntala, and both have been known to fail, not necessarily from bad translation, but from the fact that something essential is lost in the business of translation, no matter how good this may be. This applies in some measure to the comparatively modern plays of Tagore. Why?

There is no easy transition in feeling from one way of thought and feeling to another. There is no easy passage from the Sanskrit idiom of thought or language into the Anglo-Saxon idiom. Macbeth is not a universal character, but even if he were in essentials the type of man in any part of the world, whose fall is brought about through an overweening ambition, he has been conceived of as a Scot, and a Scot he will remain. He can no more be a Moor than Othello can be a Teuton.

If translation were merely a matter of words, it would not be difficult to transform the drama of a nation into drama of the world. But language is a subtle phenomenon, that is a package of traditions, all more or less subtle, reflecting thought, passion, wit, humour, tolerance or intolerance, intuition and different habits of reasoning. Unlike mathematics, it presents us with no cut-and-dried formula that can be universalised. It implies a code of morals as well as a code of manners, a code of honour as well as a code of honesty. And as the religious convictions inherent in some languages are superstitions in others at different times, it is difficult to understand how such plays as *Saint Joan* would be rendered into modern Chinese, or how *The Winslow Boy* and *Kind Hearts and Coronets* would translate into modern Russian.

Among other things a language implies a particular religious idiom. To "Western Europe, and up to a point to the United States, which has inherited this tradition of morality, the idiom of the New Testament is instinct in the language of drama. That is why it is possible to translate Shakespeare and Goethe into German and English respectively; why Moliere can be played in English (with some loss in subtlety) and why Racine and Corneille do not fall flat when played on a European stage with European theatre conventions. Try these in Indian languages with Indian theatre tradition and observe the effect. You will have translated and transported one circle of ideas into another; one way of life into another; one code, one trend of thought, one mode of reasoning into another. And to imagine that citizens of the world (if they exist) will be equally happy seeing these plays in any language, is to delude ourselves that we are nearer an international Utopia than we are ever likely to be.

The case for the translation of plays is a case for cautious judgment. As a choice between not knowing the dramatic classics of the world at all, because one does not know the language in which they were originally written, and knowing them through defective translations, one would probably prefer the latter. But one would prefer it as a *pis aller*. There is all the difference in the world between this position and the wild optimism that claims that drama has only to be assisted with international goodwill to unite the world either through the purgation of the common emotions of pity and fear, or through the common laughter that, thank heaven, we continue to share through the conflict of warring ideologies.

7

Scholarships in Educational Planning

We no longer need to argue the case for a large-scale, subcontinental award of scholarships. The Indian Constitution and the proclamation of India as a democratic Socialist State place the case for a widespread network of scholarships beyond dispute. The question is not: why scholarships? It is: how and where scholarships?

The underlying principle in the allocation of scholarships to groups and individuals is the principle of democratisation. This has all too often been taken to mean that scholarships will be awarded to the poor, irrespective of talent. On the assumption, now generally accepted, that a nation cannot survive, part-slave, part-free, there is clearly a case for a steady stream of scholarships to backward classes and communities who have to catch up with more advanced classes and communities. Nevertheless, the concept of democratisation through scholarships is not completely met by the regular award of scholarships to backward classes and communities. The true democratisation of education through scholarships is based on a principle of equity. And equity demands that scholarships will be awarded on merit to those who, for want of opportunity, are not able to do justice to their own proven potentialities or effectively, with such talents, to serve their country.

There are at least two points of view on when and to whom scholarships should be given. The old liberal conception was of a scholarship as aid to anyone of outstanding talent in a particular field, irrespective of whether or not that field served an immediate purpose in national planning. Academic merit was a sufficient reason for a scholarship. And there is something to be said for this view. It was the view probably held by such men as Michael Sadler who owe their immortal "achievement in education" to this entirely educational conception. Universities, that exist for knowledge per se and that never have been intended, under the liberal conception, to be passports to employment, to fit cogs into wheels or pegs into holes, can always be strengthened by outstanding students in the humanities or the basic sciences, who pursue knowledge for its own sake, and intend to spend their lives either in research or in teaching.

There is, however, another and at present strongly urged view that scholarships cannot be given indiscriminately for academic merit, but must be streamlined to a national educational-cum-economic plan. This need not always be at conflict with liberal practice, for no technology is possible without fundamental research, and liberal scholarships encourage fundamental research. Nevertheless, today poor countries must, it seems, have listed priorities for money-spending. Scholarships, like other assets, require to be allocated to subject-fields that, at a particular point in our history, have greater relevance in employment than other subject-fields. There are today more scholarships, internal and external, for technology than for philosophy; for science than for sociology; for medicine than for the humanities. Right or wrong, this emphasis is likely to continue as much because technology pays, as because India happens at this moment to need for her plans more engineers than she does teachers of literature or the social studies. It is in many ways a disturbing thought that the noble arts of writing and of history must yield to the making of engineers; but the history of education is likely to be increasingly punctuated by such compulsions that are of their nature, not educational but economic.

It is easier to solve individual than national problems. Democracies have always been concerned with the dignity of the individual, individual needs, abilities, aspirations. They have been educationally aware of the need to discover special talent and to prevent the waste of special abilities. Interviewing has developed into a fine art. Indeed, the whole paraphernalia of advertisement, preliminary screening on the basis of paper qualifications and professional records and a final personal interview in which academic excellence is confirmed, and merit weighed has been analysed ad nauseam and more or less perfected in execution.

Democracies have not, however, so far with conspicuous success met the requirements of a national educational plan into which scholarships can be fitted against pigeon-holes as if we were playing a game on a three-dimensional board. Perhaps, the ways of a democracy are sometimes at conflict with total planning. Nevertheless, even if we do not resort to the pigeon-hole method of training people to fit places in society, we must achieve the results of total planning. Scholarships in India have so far tended to be operated ad hoc on a rather experimental, trial-and-error method in which there has necessarily been some waste. Highly-trained scholars have sometimes returned to India to find that they have not been capable of being assimilated into the national economy. Consultation between departments of government with a view to coordinating needs with scholarships is now happily on the increase, and we may look forward to a time when waste will be, for all practical purposes, eliminated. To this end, some of the educational questions that have to be asked and answered, as scholarships are progressively integrated into an educational plan, are: (i) Where is it most necessary to award scholarships? (ii) For what period and for study to which country should scholarships be awarded?

The first is not a geographical question. It is a question of subject-fields and specialised sections of subject-fields. Where facilities for postgraduate studies or practical training already exist in India that are comparable with facilities in other parts of the world, scholarships are neither necessary nor desirable. Where facilities exist in India that are moderately good though not comparable with the best in other parts of the world, scholarships are not vitally necessary though they may at some point be desirable. "Where no facilities are available in India in subject-fields that are (a) educationally and (b) developmentally important to this country, scholarships are vital, and must be established in numbers adequate to those we require to educate.

Where shall we send Indian scholars and for what? This has largely been solved for us by the large number of scholarship offers under which educationally and industrially advanced foreign governments and organisations have made available to India places in the basic sciences, technology and the humanities. There is, indeed, the danger that where a large number of scholarships is offered by particular countries in specific fields, we will jump at them indiscriminately and without stopping to consider whether the scholarships can be put to a precise use when the scholars return to this country. We need to examine carefully all schemes that are offered us, so that we can estimate, on the educational information available, whether the country offering them has facilities not merely incomparably better than our own, but immediately adapted to equip our scholars, after training, for work in Indian conditions. This applies particularly to facilities for research and for practical training, less to facilities for teacher-training.

For how long should a scholarship be tenable? Where a scholar is potentially good material, he should be sent out of India comparatively young, i.e. say, between twenty and twenty-two. He should go for a substantial period, i.e. two to three years, preferably three years. He should not be allowed to move in quick succession from one foreign country to another but should be required to return to India to work for a period of five years before he is eligible for another scholarship abroad. Where a scholar is already advanced in years for a scholarship, i.e. when he is over twenty-five though under thirty-five, it is important to consider him for a shorter period of training, i.e. for one year and to see to it that he gets his postgraduate studies or specialised training in a field in which he can benefit from it at that stage of his professional development.

We are still groping in a large number of European countries on such matters as the precise period for which we should use scholarships, the degrees and diplomas obtainable at the end of that period and the marketability in India of these degrees and diplomas in special fields of science and technology. This is the case for evaluation. "Evaluation" is a word like "Mesopotamia" that means many things to many men. It is a word that is sometimes used fraudulently to mean anything that its user chooses it to mean. Within the context of scholarships to the individual, it is the use of his scholarship in educational as well as in practical, tangible, material terms; to the nation, it is what a scheme of scholarships brings in terms of know-how and professional leadership.

The difference that a course of study ranging over a period of three years makes to the mind of a young man is a matter that he is in some position to assess. Individual marketability is comparatively easy to estimate, for, confused as the situation is today on the large number of competing foreign degrees and diplomas, it is nevertheless clear that certain degrees and diplomas are worth more than other degrees and diplomas.

National evaluation is more difficult, partly because the intangibles increase with numbers. It is hard to know how many minds have profited in the abstract, how many skills in the mass from contact with foreign countries with varying structural patterns. Nevertheless, how important evaluation is becomes clear when we observe the number of scholars newly returned from abroad, who are either only partially employed or are not employed at all. Then, there is the inevitable maladjustment when a scholar returns home to find that his newly-won distinctions are not accepted at his own valuation, or that he is returned to the work that he was doing two or three years ago, for which his recently-won experience has now rendered him "uneconomic."

To these problems there is no easy solution, but one thing is quite certain. Unless the documentation of the cases of all scholars who do return to this country is undertaken with some system, checks made in each case on the veracity of the scholar's report, his judgments confirmed by the judgments of those with whom he works, there will be no way to define the problem for a subcontinent.

Documentation is, however, only a first step. There follows a critical analysis that is not just statistical, but that necessarily involves the use of statistics. The objective of this analysis is to see that the round peg, rendered square, is no longer forced into the round hole. Adaptability does not necessarily increase with knowledge and experience; it frequently diminishes with it, for the modern world has accepted specialisation for better or for worse, and, all knowledge, theoretical or practical, tends in that direction.

We began by saying that scholarships are educationally a good thing; but the abundance of scholarships that now sit confronting the enterprising and ambitious Indian student are also likely to become a liability if they are taken too much for granted. Several young men, well set up and comparatively of comfortable means, say: "My father can afford to send me to Britain, the USA or elsewhere; but now that there are so many scholarships available, I don't see why I shouldn't get one." There may be something to be said for this attitude if the rich young man is willing to take his chance in open competition with the poor young man. Unfortunately, this is not always so. The danger, however, lies in an attitude towards which this type of thinking tends, namely, that scholarships are a fundamental right to which all Indian nationals are entitled. This springs from another current superstition for which progressive democracy is responsible, that education is a right that may be claimed by anyone. Education at what level, pray, and for what purpose? It is difficult to see how a university education is a fundamental right in a country that has not been able to finance compulsory primary education in the span once scheduled for this educational priority.

Scholarships are not a fundamental or other right, they must be earned. And to put them too easily within the reach of young men and women who assume all too casually that being born Indian is to be entitled to such an amenity, is to emasculate and not to educate. It is to set a premium on educational complacency and to destroy scholarly initiative. A scholarship is a recognition of ability and industry that unless given "that little push forward" may decay or stand arrested, drying up those slender sources of human talent to the discovery of which educationists all over the world have pledged themselves these many centuries.

8
Rule of Three

A Fable in Letters

Dearest Romesh (ran Sushila's letter),

You will be glad to know that I have found Malati a good school. At least, that's what most people say, although most people at other times say that Delhi has no good schools at all. But, as schools go, this is a good school, and Malati seems to be happy. She's had her first report that proves that even if she isn't a scholar, she's not stupid. I think they call whatever she has "potentiality." That, at least, is what Miss Das—age 45, hair, pepper and salt (chiefly salt) eyes dim, expression severe—calls it.

I don't know many teachers. Perhaps that's what is wrong with me. Certainly, Miss Das does not approve of me. She thinks me much too vivacious, and the reason why Malati's discipline at home is "lax." She didn't say so in so many words, but her expression was more eloquent than words.

If I don't know many teachers, it seems to me that Miss Das doesn't know many parents, because I can't think I am more frivolous than most parents, and a child is surely entitled to her childhood. Nevertheless, Miss Das and I don't quite see eye to eye and I am not sure whose eye is out of focus. I should like to think it was hers.

I sometimes have a qualm of conscience because between Miss Das and me, I suppose, we preside over Malati's future. Or that's what the books and the magazines say. "Parents and teachers" they say with the earnestness of a Cassandra—"parents and teachers are directly responsible for children. There are no bad children; only bad parents." I can't help it, but frivolity keeps breaking out in me, and Miss Das is all angles. Strangely, Malati doesn't seem to think so. When I say chafingly: "Did Miss Das laugh today?" She says: "Of course, she did," and goes right on with what she is doing which leaves me feeling that perhaps my daughter is less exacting than her mother.

The long and the short of it is that Malati is in a good school and, in course of time, perhaps, Miss Das and I will be on more than nodding terms. When do you come home?

All our love,

Sushila

At about the same time Miss Das, Malati's new teacher, was writing as follows to her mother:

My dear Mother,

School has begun and with it many new children have come to us. They are like any other children, bright, not-so-bright and dull. As their teacher, it is my duty to take an interest in them all. I do my best, but I can't help remembering some and forgetting others, so that when the last exercise book is closed, the school doors bolted and the last rumble of the school bus an echo, I close my eyes and think, and I can remember Jaya, Chandra and Malati.

Malati is an entirely new girl, the other two have already been here a year though I continue to be very fond of them. Malati came to me with her mother and frankly, of the two, I prefer Malati; which means that she must have a nice and serious father. I do not mean that there is anything seriously wrong with her mother, but I think she is modern and I, old-fashioned and earnest, or that's how she makes me feel. So, when I see Malati with eyes that shine like stars and an intelligence that is only slightly less bright than her eyes, I know that she is good material. I told her mother so. Unfortunately, when I speak to her mother, I tend to use the wrong word, I wanted to tell her that her daughter was very bright indeed. Instead, I stumbled into the word "potentiality." I saw her lift her delicate brows as who should say: "You old bluestocking!"

Mother dear, that, I am afraid, is what I am. That's how you raised your daughter and I don't think that either you or I regret it. Indeed, if we had more blue-stockings with the same determination to make good students of the children who come to us, perhaps in course of time, their mothers would not look down their noses at us, would come to see us for the human beings with good intentions that we are. I should also quite seriously object to their thinking that only our intentions are good. We have a long record of service. For years, we have taught girls like Malati and have made them good, honest, clear-thinking students. If Malati doesn't shine at algebra and civics, I don't think that the world will come to an end, because she does shine at English, Hindi, history and geometry. I do my best to tell her that it is important to be an all-rounder, to use her mind on everything, but I can't quite help agreeing with her that "history is so much more interesting than geography."

I hope that you are now keeping better and that you have laid in a stock of woollen socks to protect you from the cold winds that blow. At the moment, the only cold wind that I feel is the chill of a disapproving parent.

Ever your affectionate daughter,

Bina

The subject of the foregoing letters, Malati, aged 12, wrote as follows to her friend, Lakshmi, aged 13:

Lakshmi darling,

School has begun and it is endless fun. I never saw so

many girls before; it's the nicest thing to go from a small to a big school. I only wish that you were here, I should chat with you all day long. I should tell you how I can barely wait for the school bus in the morning, that I don't like school to come to an end. Our Principal is a tall and gracious lady—even Mummy says she really is a lady. As for my teachers, they are wonderful. I like Miss Das best. She isn't young and she isn't pretty and she isn't like Miss Chanda at our last school, who was always beautifully dressed and always laughing. Miss Das does laugh but only when there's something to laugh at. I get the feeling always that she's safe and nice and "there." Do you know the feeling? She's there when you want to ask her a question, and she's there when you are puzzled, and she's there when you're really happy about something to share your fun. And she talks about history as if it were next door to you, and she reads *Pride and Prejudice* and Mr. Pickwick as if they were here at Delhi and not far, far away in England. Miss Das is homey that's why I like her. Isn't that a funny thing to say? Because if you have a nice home, and I have always been told that I have one, you shouldn't need anybody to be homey in school, should you? Mummy is always bubbling over with fun. She is very nice to laugh with, but when I am puzzled, she can't answer my questions. Then I have always to go to Miss Das. So, perhaps, it is as well to have the one for play and the other for work. What do you think?

There are many other girls here and we talk about our mothers and teachers and our fun and sometimes we compare our exercises and work out sums together. 1 don't like algebra. But the rest is very exciting and I do like Miss Das.

Love

Malati

And now, Reader, I leave you to judge for yourself the problem of these three people who have described one another and, incidentally, themselves.

9

Milestones in Educational Publishing

Most quinquennial reviews on education are heavy with fact. Assessment is generally tentative, and weighty statistical tables at the end of the volume warn the reader against rash conclusions. Fortunately, a review of the last five years in the educational publications planned, produced, published and sold by the Ministry of Education and Scientific Research need not depend for its statement on statistics. If figures appear, they do so to supplement conclusions, not to justify them.

Ten years ago, the Ministry had published about 125 publications. Most of these were State reports— annual, quinquennial or decennial—of the Central Ministry or of the States of the Indian Union. Particular parts of the country that were visited by particular officers sometimes became the subject of reviews, and frequently the reviews were discerning and valuable. But the conception of an educational publication as a pamphlet with a thesis that would be of some practical value to the practising teacher had scarcely made its appearance,

Towards the end of 1952 and early 1953 this new idea took shape. An educational publication need no longer be a stodgy bluebook. It need not necessarily be covered with figures that, when left uninterpreted for pages, can mean little to the teacher in India (or indeed anywhere in the world) and can mean less to the layman. The new educational pamphlet that was envisaged was the sort of statement that anyone could understand, who could be persuaded to read it. It had to be in a language that was easily intelligible to the secondary school teacher. It had to be practical and to take its inspiration from the educational life of the country.

Sometimes even the teacher requires just a reference book and the programme for the years that followed always included directories, handbooks, reference books in statistics and pamphlets of educational information for foreign students coming to India or for Indian students going abroad. These are part of the stock-in-trade of every educational institution and are particularly valuable for college libraries and for staff libraries of secondary schools. However, now that the educational publication need not restrict itself to recording educational progress made in this or that state, it was no longer a vehicle merely of information and a medium of educational publicity. It had and has a new function to perform.

What is this new function? It has to set the teacher thinking and to keep him thinking. It has to convert all educational full-stops (and these are very easy to come by in routine educational work) into educational question marks. The writers of these new "Studies in Education and Psychology" did not always prove their thesis to the complete satisfaction of a penetrating reader, but they always turned up new earth and in doing so caused that degree of intellectual and educational disturbance that is good for workers in this field. In the course of the next five years, the educational pamphlet and its authors made certain substantial discoveries. They discovered, for instance, that it is sometimes possible for an educational pamphlet so written as to arrest the attention of the teacher and to cause that particular disturbance that I have described as healthy for the teacher, to sell itself. It does not need the clarion cry of modern advertisement. It does not need a fiat from anywhere to make its purchase imperative.

All that it requires is that it should be intelligently conceived, easily and clearly written and reasonably well produced. It is also essential that it should be inexpensive, so that it can come within the reach of the teacher of India.

Between 1953 and 1958 we published over 275 educational works, that is to say, over twice as much as we had published in the fifteen years preceding 1952. These publications vary from the education reports for which a tradition had already been created by the end of 1952 and the statistical assessment that I have mentioned, earlier, to such new things as *Provisional and Finalised Lists of Technical Terms in Hindi, UNESCO Projects in India, Experiments in Child Education* and a string of exciting new monographs such as *The Single-Teacher School, Vidya Bhavan Open-Air Session, Research and Experiment in Rural Education, and Child Art*, the Ministry's first pictorial publication designed to interest and assist teachers of art and to entertain children.

This was a first step in the right direction and it was followed by a series of other steps that widened the fan-line pattern of the educational publications programme and intensified its value. One of these *was Seven Years of Freedom* brought out in 1954, that was a bird's-eye view of progress made in various branches of education since 1947; another, *Student Indiscipline* in English and Hindi, a third, *Experiments in Teacher-Training* and a fourth, *Better Teacher Education*. There followed *The Content of History in Indian Schools, Understanding Basic Education, The Five-Year Plan, Schemes of Educational Development, and The Five-Year Plan—A Brief Review of Progress, Self-Reform in Schools; A Report by Working Educators,* and *Headmasters on Secondary Education.*

In the last two publications more new ground was broken, for at last the working teacher was provided with a platform and could speak on developments in his own profession. Verbatim reports were kept of two seminars and the results when printed were used by the teachers and headmasters who attended the seminars for the benefit of colleagues in their own schools. Much later when the Ministry ran symposia in its main periodical *The Education Quarterly* (that it later issued as separate publications under such titles as *These Schools are Ours* and *My Idea of a University*), the teacher spoke forthrightly as the expert that he is. At last he was able to offer the country his own practical experience which is the most valuable of all educational counsel.

I have described the development of educational publications as a fan-time movement. A fan consists of a certain number of fine pleats that are revealed as the handle opens the fan out. This is clear as we move down our five years to the present day. Increasing awareness of rural education gave rise first to "Rural Institutes" and later to a monograph on "The Rural Primary Teacher" in English and Hindi. Then, confusions and misunderstandings on Basic Education and the programme for Basic Education stimulated such publications as *The Concept of Basic Education, Bibliography on Basic Education, Handbook for Teachers of Basic Schools* (in Hindi and English), *Report of the Assessment Committee on Basic Education* (Hindi and English), *Orienting Primary Schools Towards the Basic Pattern* (Hindi and English) and *Seminar on Basic Education*.

Child Art had opened a new field of study—Studies of Culture-in-Education. This was followed presently by Child Writing, that consisted of the experimental writing of children between the ages of four and sixteen in various countries of the world and over a period of three years, *Playwriting and Playmaking*, which was an introduction to drama for university students, and *The Film as an Educational force in India*. One of the main pleats in the educational fan is the book that caters in a rather special way for the practising teacher and on this there have been two—*The Teacher We Need in India Today* and *The Teacher in India Today*. The first sold out in three months; the second sold very well.

Before 1953 the educational bestseller was unknown in India. That is no longer so. A "bestseller" in education requires definition, for our editions do not ordinarily exceed 5,000 though some have print orders of 12,000 and 15,000. But pamphlets that run into two or three reprints or editions in one year may, it seems, with some justification, be regarded as educational bestsellers. This has now happened with several publications. It has happened with *Teachers' Handbook of Social Education,* with *Scholarships for Studies Abroad,* with *The Single Teacher School* and with *Student Indiscipline.*

That these publications and periodicals are read is testimony to the fact that educational journalism in India is now a force to reckon with. That the public demands more and more of the sort of educational publication that I have described is good news for all teachers, writers, editors and publishers of enterprise. It is especially good news because we have needed for some years a common platform on which these people shall meet to coordinate their complementary thinking and activity.

10
Remembered Why?

There is an air of preciosity about the dwindling generation of Indians who went either as a matter of course or by accident up to either of the old English universities. Indians in general resent their air of belonging to a superior club; Americans in general resent the notion that either of these universities is relevant to the complicated business of 1963. And so, I ask myself, why Indians who, between the twenties and the sixties of this century, went up to Oxford or Cambridge, remember so well what should now have become a distant and vague experience.

The heart of the matter is that the two old universities that Britain gave itself and the world were more than a passing experience for those of us who experienced them at the right time in the growing years. They shaped and conditioned us for work and for life. They conferred upon us not learning and knowledge only, but a way of thought, a way of service.

Whether or not that way of thought and service is adequate to the strenuous demands of the 1960s is a matter that has now to be examined by those who have such an experience within their reach. What is it that the two old British universities gave Indians that is so important to our being, living, and doing in the sixth decade of the 20th century?

In the first place, and let us make no mistake about it, they gave us academic standards. There was a minimum in learning, thinking, presentation, below which you could not afford to fall if you were to remain up at either Oxford or Cambridge. Failure was not fashionable; it was sad and regrettable. Frivolity, that went beyond the day-to-day flippancy, was not an accomplishment. There was laughter, and in abundance, because laughter is a necessary ingredient of the growing years. It is that which gives proportion to seriousness, and restores proportion when it has been lost through self-importance, solemnity, or an excess of power. But, or perhaps because so much of the experience came to you through laughter, it was seen to be of deep seriousness. No one who ever enjoyed his residence at either Oxford or Cambridge suffered from the illusion that life up at either was undiluted fun.

The notion that these universities do not exact work but are satisfied with showmanship, is one that must be abandoned in our more realistic times. Oxford and Cambridge demand hard work of anyone up to take a good Honours degree. People who are content with a Pass degree are automatically consigned to an inferior category of undergraduate. The university exists to promote scholarship. All standards derive from scholarship. Integrity is defined, discerned, recognised through and by scholarship. Personality is larger than scholarship, but the accent at both universities was, and still appears to be, an accent on scholarship.

India is still sufficiently scholarly of practice (she was always scholarly of tradition) to understand that scholarship and showmanship do not normally go together. I am not running down showmanship, which has its uses. I am merely seeking to establish that there is no necessary or natural connexion between them. In the study of the Humanities, there may be other places as good for scholarship as Oxford, but there can be few places more competent to define the purpose of study, the method and manner of study best designed to produce a good mind for Literature, Language or the Social Studies.

The idea that Oxford and Cambridge are concerned with things outside scholarship, that are less deserving of acquisition, springs from the fact that residential life provides, apart from learning, for enjoyment. This is so. But there is nothing in the residential life of either university that need divert the undergraduate from his work. Indeed, university societies are intended to complement, to round off the work of tutorials, lectures and private study. This they do admirably. The formal seminar had come to stay at Oxford over twenty years ago. University societies provide students with that informal seminar which is probably more effective because more memorable. These societies imply that the student shall keep abreast of the latest writing on his subject. If, he has not done so, he will be found out or reduced to a position of inferiority by those of his own years who are more knowledgeable. Discussions, lectures, the intellectual sword-play of argument and repartee at these meetings in subjects allied to a special subject, help to bring ideas home, to enlarge them, to demonstrate the many-sidedness of knowledge, people, and life. That all this is done with enjoyment is surely not a matter for regret. Indeed, this is one reason why life at the residential universities is so memorable.

The other argument generally urged even two decades ago, and urged more persistently today, is that life at both Oxford and Cambridge is unreal, no preparation for life in a modern, keenly competitive society. A university was never intended, any more than a school or college was intended, to be life in miniature. Indeed, the special attraction of life at a university, any university, is that it does not reflect the everyday life that can come to be depressing, distressing, chaotic, and exacting for the wrong reasons. A university is a place to which students in the growing years, generally between 17 and 23 go to learn to think for themselves. They do not learn to live, they acquire the thinking habits (and I hope, the sensibility) whereby they will have to live their later and earning lives. That either Oxford or Cambridge handicapped a man or woman to earn his or her living in India at any time, then or now, has to be proven. Twenty years is a long time in which to test out the ideas that you inherited from a university. That you have not had radically to revise these ideas when the world has sped as swiftly as it has, is surely a tribute to the enduring character of the approach to learning and living that an old English university gave.

But what did Oxford teach that has been so valuable in India in the last twenty years? It taught that there is no substitute for truth and for the integrity that proceeds from truthfulness or that is apiece with it. It taught that only the truly serious can be truthful. It taught that the sin against truth is the sin against life.

Strangely, no one sat down to say these things. It was in the air of every room, of every college, of every university, of every tutorial, lecture, discussion, and debate. All tradition proclaimed it, all ambition converged on it. This did not rule out either goodness or beauty; it brought both nearer truth. There is certainly some ugliness at Oxford, but it tends to be nearer 'town' than 'gown'. That some part of the prosperity of the university is derived from the materialistic town is not to be denied. However, within the precincts of the university there is no quality so highly prized as truthfulness. This is the exaction that dominates the whole life of Oxford, and it is the gospel with which everyone who has been touched by the university goes down into the world to preach by example.

The immediate concomitant of this truthfulness is unworldliness. You have to live and work in the world, but to replace what you have learnt about the dominant importance of truthfulness by the god of getting-on is to deny everything that you have been taught. There is no law against success; no adage that warns a man to prefer failure. Not at all. For the universities have had a crop of great leaders in many nations, in many different fields, and have not failed to recognise them with some of that proprietorial pride with which a university may legitimately regard its distinguished alumni. All that Oxford and Cambridge warn a man and a woman against in their implicit lesson of deep seriousness and deep truthfulness, is the acceptance of worldly success or the pursuit of it at the expense of integrity. Everything that lies at the heart of Oxford's greatness is inextricably bound up with the habit of unworldliness. It is her pearl of great price, her talisman against corruption.

Why are these universities remembered by Indians twenty, years later so well, so deeply, with a sense not of gratitude only but of reverence? And that, long after an Indian university to which we went before going abroad is forgotten?

The answer is, I think, that Oxford and Cambridge gave, and give, what our universities do not yet give after a hundred years— not merely a habit of mind, of study, an art of presentation or showmanship, but a code of thinking and living. Many Indian undergraduates have lost faith in their traditional religions, but still have an ethic that is not derived from religion per se. Look for the source of the ethic that makes them live honourable lives. It should proceed from a school, a college and, most of all, from a university. The two old British universities had the capacity to confer this code on those who drank deep of their waters. The code became so intricate a part of you that you did not stop to think that it was foreign, remote, or acquired. It is the attitude of mind and spirit with which you rise each morning, live and work each day, go to sleep each night. There is no time-table for its operation; no Sabbath for its periodic display. It is hidden in the innermost recesses of the lives of those who used well their years at the old universities.

These are the things that Indians need to live their strenuous lives in the 1960s and these things many of us draw from the old British universities. Not till the universities of India have won a comparable hold over the minds and imaginations of students, not till they have become an intrinsic part of the breathing, living, unconscious man and woman of India, will they have served the Indian nation as well as those distant, foreign universities of Oxford and Cambridge.

11

The Essential Teacher

If, in a fling of fun, the gods decided to send Socrates back to earth and, in another fling, sent him to India, which supposedly he had not visited earlier, what would he say to them all—the educational planners, the administrators and teachers?

There really is no knowing; but almost certainly he would take them all, question by question, to the heart of the matter, which is the essential teacher. "Planning", he might begin by saying, "is, according to you, a way of making India safe for educating children. Is it possible to make India safe for all her children, unless you have decided on the kind of teacher who can do this for you? For, much as I admire educational planners, administrators and all that", the sage might go on dreamily, "would you agree that without creating the essential teacher, they really cannot work their plans?" And so on.

Within ten minutes of his arrival in our subcontinent, he would have got to the heart of the business that so many of us shirk: that educational planning is still so concerned about numbers, that it makes no deliberate provision for the pursuit of excellence. It does not say to itself: unless we have this and this kind of teacher, our plans to educate India will go awry.

But to this uncomfortable conclusion, Socrates would drive us; and if one of us blundered into saying, "We can have at one and the same time both quantitative education and quality, one would see the eye that burned, yes, literally burned, light up once again to teach that at any given point of time you will, with limited human and financial resources, have either democratic education or good education. For the teacher, who is the heart of the business, is finite, inelastic and geographically a fixed point. And to other educationists who murmured: "There are always teaching aids", Socrates might reply: "I understood an aid to be that which is added to a teacher, and does not subsist by itself, but I may of course be wrong. The only difference between us", he might twinkle, "is that I know that I know nothing".

And so he would drive us back to the wall with: "What in your judgment is the essential teacher?" Only by looking hard at him and the procession that he leads in the story of teaching, shall we have the glimmerings of an answer to this question, that is so vital to the preservation of quality in education.

What is the essential teacher? It starts possibly with Socrates, possibly earlier, but it will do to begin with Socrates, and then, (not being too particular about chronology, for this is an eclectic study) to see the tall heads and the broad shoulders that make up the procession of teachers through the ages over the wide world—Socrates, Thomas Aquinas, Ascham and Aylmer, Comenius, Rousseau, Pestalozzi, Froebel, Bronson Alcott, Horace Mann, Freud, William James, Tilak, Dewey, Gokhale, Annie Besant, Tagore, Maria Montessori, Karve, Conant.

They were no one country's monopoly, these men and women, and none of them was a notably happy person. How, indeed, should he be, or she be, when they were constantly voices of protest against a mob of comfortable agreement? Here, for instance, was Bronson Alcott in Connecticut, trying in the first stages of his teaching to be conventional, and to do as his patrons wanted. From his home he went to Boston. And then a strange thing happened. He became a thinking teacher, one who had views of his own and felt them strongly enough to press them regardless of the consequences. He took a negro girl into his school. He talked in and out of season of the 'almighty wall' that he intended to make and keep beautiful, for beauty and learning, he saw, are positively connected.

He grew, thought his patrons, wilder and wilder. And certainly he was as wildly enlightened as was his forbear, Socrates. Finally, they decided that he was altogether too original for them. They ganged up against him. Alone, Alcott faced his enemies, and was seemingly driven by them from the only teaching position he could get. So he fades out of educational history. Or does he?

There was Froebel, who tried one thing after another, 'an unsuccessful, gloomy, morbid man this, with the hand of the world against him, but in love with small children. He wandered about the fields and the country roads, hammering out his own ideas and his own methods of teaching, and one fine day on a country walk: "Eureka !" he cried "I have it. My school for little ones will be called *kindergarten*." And so the beloved word was born.

He had better luck now than ever before. A Baronness, a strange woman who thought that it was better to be busy than baronial, joined him, and from her papers we get gleanings of how this genius thought and worked to make children love learning. And all this he did regardless of the consequences.

There was Father Pestalozzi, as ugly as Socrates, ragged, unkempt, absent-minded, who gathered poor children round him, and wrote as madly as he spoke, also regardless of the consequences. Strange ideas emerged from this ragged old man, for he talked now of the school being part of the community, and the community as reflecting the school. They were bound imdissolubly together, and if you wanted your community to be educated, you must make the connection clear in your planning, for a total community, rich and poor. For (though he did not say so then, he would have said so today) if you have decided upon compulsory primary education, you must take the consequences in educated unemployment unless you can tailor your total national plans successfully to absorb all those you educate at primary level.

There was Rousseau who taught for his times the startling truth, that there is no mind that is not shaped by the emotions, that the child you teach is not a mere brain into which you instil willy-nilly the formulae and facts of academica, but a total person made of hands, organs, dimensions, feelings. And he, too, taught regardless of the consequences. How could he know that there would follow in his footsteps a man called Freud? But that is another story.

And Socrates, looking, at the procession that followed him, might at some point say: "What do you think the essential teacher is?" It seems to me that the only answer that he would accept without a further question in that nagging way of his, is: "The essential teacher is he who has something to say, that he has thought out for himself, hacked out of his own experience, recognising solemnly that this is better than a place in the bazaar or the comforts of power." For the man who persistently concentrates upon the examined life regardless of the consequences is no more, no less, than the direct descendant of Socrates himself.

12
Any Parent to Any Teacher

Dear Teacher,

There is a superstition that all parent-teacher relations are efforts in peaceful coexistence. So far am I from sharing this popular misconception, that I am writing to tell you without preliminary that I think that you and I have the same job to do in educating my 15-year old-daughter, Zia.

Zia is bent on studying history; it appears from the fact that you have chosen to teach history, that you are bent on teaching it. I am bent on seeing the transmission of ideas, attitudes and knowledge from you to her. It is possible, though unlikely, that you and I differ on the business of history and on methods of teaching. This, however, is not the main point. The main point is that we should be agreed that history is an essential part of anyone's education in 1970, and that women have much to gain by studying it as a discipline and delight.

Which leads me to want to compare notes with you on where we are going in the daily business of educating our children. Because (1) your classes are as large as they are, it is possible that, though you know that Zia is in your class of 40, you may not know her either as an individual or as an individual bent on reading history. Also (2), having got to know her, you may find that you have to supplement, correct or modify much that she brings to you from her home.

Strangely, though a parent is not handicapped by point (1), she is often handicapped, as is a teacher, by point (2). For the home has, I think, as often to supplement, correct or modify the environment and influence of a school, as vice versa.

In this rather intricate scheme of relationships, I am generally more sympathetic to the teacher than to the parent, but only because, whereas it is possible to choose a teacher for one's daughter, it is not possible to choose a parent for one's pupil. Parents are the datum with which children, schools and teachers have to work. They are sometimes intractable material, more often responsive, and sometimes, handsomely cooperative. I have a hunch, too, that the handsomely co-operative parent is made, not born; and that she or he is made by an imaginative teacher.

The long and the short of this philosophical excursion is that both of us are indissolubly associated through your student, and my daughter. Of the two of us, you will see Zia's abilities perhaps more justly, less sympathetically than I. I will see her talents to the possible exclusion of her potentialities. For affection such as most mothers instinctively have for most daughters confers, in addition to information, the insight that is infinitely more valuable than information.

For some time to come, you and I may not meet. This may not be necessary. For you, I know, are a heavily burdened professional woman and I, for my part, have a well-scheduled day of work and play in which I try to avoid unnecessary meetings. I would, however, enjoy meeting you some time and that, sooner than later. 1 am not writing to make an appointment, for you cannot know my daughter well enough yet to discuss her or to plan for her improvement. There may, however, come a time when it will be a pleasure and profit for me to meet you, and then I will be grateful for your candid opinion of what you think is right, and what is wrong about Zia's present attitudes. For these, surely, are a good deal more important in the business of education than the volume of information that she has been able to imbibe in her not-very-long life.

If, before the meeting to which I look forward, you should wish to get in touch with me for any reason, do, please, feel free to write to me or to ring me. In the meanwhile, I hope that Zia will be to you in some part, what she has been to me these last 15 years, a source of growing happiness.

Educationally Yours,
Muriel Wasi

13

The Case of the Educated Woman

The case of the educated woman is a problem that faces us here and now in India.

Who is she, the educated woman of India? Some tangible definition that makes location easy is, it seems, necessary for our discussion and her utility. The educated woman in India is a woman with at least a first degree of a university or other recognised institution of higher education. Such women, it will be argued, are of dubious academic merit or practical use, and certainly the average woman with a first degree from many Indian universities leaves something to be desired on both counts.

It will also be argued that there are women without these qualifications who are both worthwhile and useful. This, too, must be admitted for there are some, though not many, women who occupy sigaificant positions in India today, who are without a university degree. They exist in social work, politics, journalism and allied fields at pretty high levels of responsibility. They cannot be entirely ignored.

The answer to these two arguments respectively is, I think, that by and large the Indian woman with a first degree of a university, bad as she is no worse than an Indian man with the same qualification, and he appears to be considered worthy of employment. The definition that we have accepted applies generally; exceptions must always be conceded to exist

A few years ago it was probably true to say that the educated working women of India had the best of two worlds—the world of constitutional equality and the world of chivalry that most Indian men in the offices of big cities still have. Inevitably this position of privilege has altered with keener competition and the recognition by men that women are rivals, and well-educated women, dangerous rivals.

Chivalry does not die overnight; it is merely, as time goes on, noticeably less chivalrous. A woman is not today, always or often, or even generally the constant emblem of nobility, fidelity, acquiescence that the country supposed that it had inherited. She is, being educated, clear-sighted and understands her rights and capacities. She is ambitious and fights for her place in the sun. She is responsible and accepts the challenge of competition with men with whom, in certain fields, she can more than hold her own. It is not to be wondered at that, with this advancing, articulate force, chivalry has given place by degrees to, first, suspicion, then caution and, finally, ruthlessness.

Can our educated women take this? I believe that they can, and the better educated and trained they are (for education and training are not the same thing) the better their chance of permanent survival. For this is precisely what they are now fighting for— permanent survival with a status and powers commensurate with their education, qualifications, training and ability.

Women in India with a postgraduate qualification of any kind, humanistic or technological, are in some definable ways superior to men with similar qualifications. The days are gone when the immobility or other physical helplessness of an educated Indian woman can be used as an argument for withholding from her a responsible appointment in public life.

The educated woman of today willingly accepts the penalty of not being mobile or independent, which is not to be employed at all. There is, however, a certain unwillingness today to part power to women at the very highest rungs of administration.

The argument plausibly advanced that, as the mass of men at present employed at senior levels, have not served under women, discipline under women will be less good than it is at present, rings hollow. Almost certainly such arguments were used by men in the progressive countries of the world in which a woman today has, in fact as well as theory, equal status with men of the same qualifications, experience and training. Yet these countries have accorded to their women responsibility such as is wielded by men, seemingly without a calamity.

The unwillingness in India to part at senior levels with power and responsibility to women springs of a known mixture of inherited malaise at the prospect of petticoat government, and from genuine and not understandable masculine envy.

One of the truly distressing things for India today is that practically no documentation has been done on how many educated women are employed profitably or suitably; how many are employable but unemployed; how many are maladjusted by qualification and training for the work they now do; what the potential is for voluntary service of this extremely valuable section of the Indian population; what proportion of women in the big cities are able and willing to render voluntary service; what machinery should be brought into being to achieve, first, the necessary documentation, and next, placement for both paid and voluntary work.

Till this documentation is done by a responsible body with preferably the ability to make its findings available readably to the nation, we shall be in no position to solve the case of the educated woman of India, and it will go by default. A survey such as the one described requires to be carried out urgently. It would reveal significant figures. More, it would reveal qualifications, abilities, training, experience that might well reduce many men in senior positions in public life today to shame. Add to this, the special qualities in public service for which educated women have long been known—conscientiousness, dependability, dedication—and it is clear that not to use the educated woman of India to the hilt of her employability is to deny not only her, but the entire Indian nation a treasure more precious than Solomon's rubies or, more topically, than Indian gold.

14

The Myth of the Average Child

One of the more curious absurdities of misreading the implication of a democracy the size of India is that a new version of "Hunt-the-slipper" or "Hot-beans-cold-butter-come-and-find-my-lady's supper" is now played in mock-educational circles. Curriculum-makers more enthusiastic than wise, educational publicists mistaking large print orders in the English language for democracy on the march, talk of catering for the "average" child. Who is this child in a sub-continent the size of a country like India, that still has wide contrasts between her urban and rural areas and a deeply stratified society that defies, in the short run, the equalisation of opportunity?

If "average" is to have a precise connotation, the average child of India must be sought and found in a rural area. With about 80 per cent of our children in these areas it would be hard to escape the conclusion that the hunted "slipper" or "my lady's supper" are both located far from the big cities of a developing society.

Yet to seek to cater for such (rural) children in the English language in vast print orders is an absurdity that it does not take a fastidious degree of education to recognise. Once talk of the "average" child in terms of the English language, and automatically you have moved away from the mathematical average that lives in the depths of rural India, and into urban and semi-urban societies that have some acquaintance with modernity and the flavour of the still swiftly-growing English language.

The question requires to be re-phrased. Who is the "average" child of India who is capable of reading a book in living-and-growing English? Here again there is no easy answer because the question implies an egalitarian condition that does not yet exist in our country.

For the linguist who surveys India today in terms of the degree of excellence achieved at school level in the use of English, never was there a country more elusive than India. There is every variety of imperfection in the use of the English language, as there is still, surprisingly, some degree of excellence, among secondary school-going children in India who use the English language either as a medium of instruction or as a field of study. To discover an average, even if one has restricted the area of search to Calcutta, Bombay, Madras, Delhi and such towns as Bangalore, Hyderabad and Nagpur, is still extremely difficult.

Those eager to locate the "average" child in English are on a wild goose chase. He/she does not exist in terms of the English language. It is reasonable, logical and sensible to locate the average child in a pre-determined group that is a locatable socio-economic unit with a given educational tradition. The number of provisos here involved points up the difficulty of identifying such a person and of establishing that he/she constitutes a standard or point of reference.

But why is it so important to locate such a body? Because it is assumed wrongly that educational democracy implies big print orders in books, subjecting all children to the same burden of mediocrity. Large print orders are justified only because, other things being equal, they reduce the price per copy, and democracy in India implies inexpensive educational literature. A textbook must unfortunately cater for as many children as possible. This is not true of enrichment of supplementary educational materials in which doctrinaire large print orders are bad education and bad economics. They are bad education because they do nothing but depress bright children who are national assets. They are bad economics because they tend to retard the development even of the not-so-bright and prevent their becoming national assets.

It is hazardous to attempt educational publications in this hit-or-miss fashion that assumes, but has not established, that the average English-reading child today is a linguistic moron who must never be fed with what is likely to stretch him More: in national terms it is wasteful/to overlook the high percentage of bright children in every assemblage of urban and semi-urban children who are ambitious to attempt work that is beyond their immediate attainments.

It is not surprising, though it is ironical, that the loudest claims about the "average" child come from people with minimal experience of teaching at school level, who are untrained in methods of evaluating such materials and who have, in any case, so dubious a command of the living English language that they cannot (for instance) see that such a book as Orwell's *Animal Farm* could be suitable for several different grades of a secondary schools. Not all these grades would get the same out of the novel, but this would not justify its exclusion from a level that did not perceive its full subtlety. 1 have watched children of nine in the big cities read *Animal Farm* with pleasure as an animal story. The same children have read it at 15 as a subtle political parable. In my view, it was suitable for both lots of children for different reasons. The "average" in each group differed substantially. It would have been incorrect to say that it suited an "average" child of 15 but not of nine. The crucial question is: An average of 15 where? Under what circumstances? With what traditions? With what abilities in language? These questions many of our people have never asked and answered.

This article is a plea for greater care in the use of the word "average", in educational discussion. It is not always possible to qualify statements with provisos in the manner of a lawyer speaking to a brief. But to use "average" with the looseness with which the non-educational (and even some teachers, who should know better) use it, is infinitely worse. To do this misleads entire populations of parents waiting to be advised on what is good for their children. It reduces the quality of writing to what was considered not long ago a sample of sub-normal work in the secondary classroom. It assumes, what it has no right to assume, that the more barren the writing, the more intelligible it is, which is patently untrue.

It is wiser in education to aim at a point higher than a child's attainment than at a point within his easy grasp. Children are easily bored with books that contain no challenge, that do not introduce them to new ideas, that patronise them, and that make no demands of them in referencing and further reading.

There is no "average" child in the subcontinent of India who is willing and eager to read in the English language. The average has meaning only in pre-defined groups. To depress this average with too-easy reading in English is much more unwise than to assume that it can work, with its teachers (and there are no average teachers either in the big cities of India) towards a standard of which it is potentially and, in the short run, completely capable.

15

Censorship and the Adolescent

If psychology is to be let loose on censorship, there is no knowing the range of evil that will be discovered in a comparatively innocent censor. There is, however, little doubt that much censorship that is at present exercised in India, is exercised either superfluously or misguidedly. Some reconsideration is overdue on what the censor's business is, and what scope should be allowed him for the exercise of his functions in the interest of society and the adolescent. Failing this, the principle should generally be recognised that censorship is best when it is least censorious.

The most healthy function of all censorship since the world began is the protective function. We are always aware of the difference between the strength of experience and that of innocence. Undoubtedly in rare cases, innocence has an armour of its own, but normally it must be protected. Adolescence, that is so resentful of the imputation of innocence, is, in effect, often more innocent than childhood.

Censorship in books and in films for adolescents cannot, it seems to me, be whittled down or out of existence. There is a case for it, but this is a field in which intelligence is more necessary than morality, and errors more frequent in commission than omission.

The adolescent is in the unhappy stage of betwixt-and-betweenness in which knowledge is sought and curiosity stimulated, without the strength to bear the burden of knowledge or the wisdom to curb the passion for curiosity. In consequence, it is as well not to withhold knowledge but to present it seasonably.

There is so much knowledge that can, and should be given to adolescents, that adults are afraid to give them, because they have not the wit to know how to present such material. This is one reason why an Index, weighs so heavily on books, and why film censorship works its ragged, capricious and irrational way on films that adolescents might well see without suffering great harm.

Unless we accept and proceed to work on the theory that writing for adolescents, is a specialised occupation in which both men and women have to be trained, first, to know adolescents, and then, to entertain them, we shall make the laborious mistake of having to screen a large volume of literature written for adults, in order to see what part of it is suitable for adolescents.

In this case, prevention means setting up bodies of people as informally as possible, to understand what adolescents want to read and need to read, and these are not always the same thing. Once we have discovered such bodies of people, and they are generally mothers or fathers or teachers of adolescent boys and girls, there will be no need to go in for the full-scale rabid censorship that now afflicts adolescent literature.

But since the process of discovering creative artists is always slow and sometimes impossible we have to begin somewhere pretty soon, and the way to begin is to place in charge of book censorship (if this is necessary, where it is necessary) people who have the best interests of adolescent-entertainment at heart. A good adage in these times is: "Look after adolescent entertainment, and instruction will look after itself."

This applies equally to films. If one considers the number of research theses on juvenile delinquency, one is driven to the belief that delinquents are always made, never born. In itself this is doubtful, because heredity plays, it would seem, almost as important a part in delinquency as environment. Undoubtedly, however, it is optimistic to think that by correcting an environment, we can eliminate delinquency or reduce it and as, in education it is always necessary to be optimistic, we can proceed to hope that environmental delinquency can be cured in some measure by wise administration in adolescent films.

The adolescent imitates almost as much as the child does—but with a difference. The thing to imitate is sophistication, and this sophistication has to be evident enough for the adolescent to perceive it, so that he or she will achieve some success in the process of imitation.

Gangster films, it seems, are less productive of delinquency than other films that make a more subtle appeal to subterranean qualities in adolescents, not always seen and, therefore, not always deplored. I would be less hard on the gangster film than on the film for girls that insidiously encouraged a "harem" habit of mind or taught a girl to exploit her femininity in order to win easy success. This is precisely what a large number of weak-minded adolescent girls want to be told, and if they find that adults are in a mood to encourage such an attitude, they feel that they have a moral sanction for what their baser inclinations commend.

This is only one small example to show that censorship of books and films for adolescents needs to be re-thought out in a more modern, more unorthodox and rational way, in order to protect innocence, not so much from itself, as from the calculated experience of the box office.

16

The Lion and the Censor

Censorship in India normally errs by being over-enthusiastic. It works zealously in favour of caution, protection and harmony, against audacity, independence, disharmonic revelation. So that when a film like *The Lion* comes along, and is preceded by a book with a child-heroine, that is supposedly absorbing fare for children, we know that the censor is going to slip up in the opposite direction. He omits to be cautious to protect and to achieve harmony: he passes the film for universal exhibition.

The Lion is superficially a film to hold children from play. In fact it has the effect of holding old men (and women) from the chimney corner. For here is a film with all the ingredients of human complexity. Certainly, there is a child at the centre and heart of it. But the child reflects in a frightening way the mistakes of two men and a woman. The mistakes cohere and jump to make of the child an incipient fascist.

To all appearance this child is normal. She is gay, carefree, lithe as a gazelle as she leaps about the jungle that is her adopted home. She has the normal human emotions towards her mother whom she loves, and her stepfather, who has taught her to love him. She has the child's affection for African servants and she adores a lion cub, that has since grown up and is now "King" in more senses than his small mistress can guess.

And yet, and yet...one is aware quite early on in the film that this is no ordinary child. For one thing, she is abnormally intelligent. She has learnt her jungle lore from a celebrated hunter, her step-father. She has, as if she were a girl-Mowgli, an instinct about life in the jungle that no mere adult can emulate. She can interpret an unnatural stillness in the forest as she can sense a break in the normal rhythm of its life. Her whole springing sympathy with the way of the jungle is dictated both by her native intelligence and the second sense that she has acquired from her step-father and her environment. This is the only world that she has ever known.

But Tina (for that is her name) is also a child of abnormal sensibility and, more than anything else in the world, she has wanted and missed the love of her own father, "Animals don't leave their young", she apostrophises the laggard father when she meets him, and that is her last word. To his desertion of her as a baby, she reacts with the passion of a child abnormally intelligent and abnormally sensitive. She cannot forgive him. The rage, that is the other face of love, possesses her and drives her to punish him. So she leads him into the trap of meeting King, now a full-grown lion, when he, all-unsuspecting, has imagined that he is going to meet a man or a harmless pet. Over King, she presides like a fascist chief, crying hysterically again and again that he will do whatever she tells him to do, be quiet or kill. She threatens and ridicules her father, like the caricature of a tyrant that she has become. When she sees her mother kiss the man who has deserted her as a small child, she is racked with a jealousy that is akin to the anguish of a woman. She confides in King, and possibly in her step-father, but not in her mother. None of this is for children.

Even less for a child-audience is the critical moment when King has to choose between, the mate that he has just taken, and the girl-child with whom he has grown up. True to nature, he chooses the lioness. Harrowed by this second desertion, the child runs after them, and only when she is at the point of being killed by the lioness, does King intervene, responding apparently to his old fidelity, to save her. But the whole scene gives those who understand it, furiously to think—and to fear.

But there is more to follow. In the horrifying scene in which the new African Chieftain, as sinister of looks as of purpose, is to take over from the old, Tina is one with the wild beat of the drums that portend murder. She is in love with violence, without compassion for old age. She has learnt all too well the lesson of the jungle, that survival implies strength. She despises weakness, rejoices in every manifestation of might. All her young passion is with the living and the mighty, against age, sickness and weariness. Savagery has entered her blood and taken possession of her mind.

Surely, this strange map of emotions, some abnormally adult, some necessarily young and childish, is not a fit subject for children. For adolescents, who understood vaguely that a child had been made the arena for a battle of emotions between two men and a woman, this must have been a frightening study. Smaller children cannot have understood it—it can have done them neither harm nor good. But to miss the point is to miss the film. Here, photography—and this is always excellent—and the love of a child for an animal, is not a substitute for understanding this most adult, sophisticated and subtle study of the power of experience to corrupt innocence and to torment it. Yet this is precisely where censorship should operate. To defend innocence from experience, to see that it is not exposed to sexual strife till it can deal with it......this is what the business of censorship is about.

17

Education and Traditional Values*

It is easier to keep water flowing as it has always done than to re-direct a channel: it is easier to move with than against the tide. The older the country in which you live and learn, the sooner you realise that the easiest way to live is to agree; the most abiding thing to learn is what your fathers taught. Tradition appears to need no defence. It has stood the hardest of all tests, the tests of Time that includes history, with succeeding waves of revolution and reaction, enchantment, disenchantment and re-enchantment with inherited values. In such countries as ours the last word resembles the first more nearly than it does any of those valuable intermediate words upon which discussion turns and hangs and upon which (so it seems to me) the present and the future of Education rest.

Are we agreed on the basic question of what Education is? There is bound to be pretty general international agreement on what it is not, and I hope that by 1962 the peoples of the world are agreed that Education is not the accumulation of information in this or that culture or study or ology or social or physical science or fine art. Information is an aid to the educationist. It builds up a language that makes the birth and growth of ideas possible; but it does not provide him with

---

* Paper presented at a Seminar called by the Indian National Commission for Cooperation with UNESCO.

the tools of thought. Those lie elsewhere in the evolution of a reasoning process and technique, the steady growth of the imagination, the sharpening of insight till the point at which, thrusting aside the pedestrian movement from fact to fact Gradgrind-wise, the student sees to the heart of the matter in a leap at once intuitive and logical, for all intuition is ultimately fed by the logic of centuries. The function of education now, then and always is to make men, women and children think clearly, think steadily, think deeply and think truly. This implies the ability to distinguish between the real that is the rational, and the real that is not susceptible of rational explanation, the notion that has been acquiesced in without scrutiny and the abiding certitude that is greater than the certainties of measurement. In this process there is room for reason and imagination, for logic and intuition, for intelligence and understanding. In it, there is no room for acceptance on faith, for reverence on and through emotion, for devotion through mysticism to the customs of ages that are perhaps picturesque, but do not stand up to the clear-eyed scrutiny of ruthless honesty.

Tradition sits upon us in India today with a complacency that is frightening to all young educationists and paralysing to those, like me, who are in the middle years. A part of our tradition is reverence for inherited ideas, way of thought and life, for the guru full of years who is presumed also to be full of honours, for age and experience, against youth and experiment.

This is a forthright plea for the rejection upon reason of reverence in Education, and for the acceptance as imperative educationally of the habit of critical thought.

To convert the fullstops of ages into question-marks is the first step towards getting men, women and children in the Indian subcontinent to prepare the ground for modern education. Blind faith starts with religion of all kinds, sometimes basically grand because it appeals to that which is larger than men, sometimes less grand because it is involved in a mesh of ritual and leads to an unthinking exclusiveness. This is true, more or less, of all the religions of India today and of the persisting bias in education that favours faith against criticism. In itself neither is good; both require to be examined.

I do not suggest that all spiritual problems are resolved by reason. I suggest that to hold credos without subjecting them constantly to the scrutiny of reason is always dangerous and sometimes dishonest. For belief is a kind of refuge for the unthinking. It provides that psychological and ethical citadel upon which the blows of reason leave no mark, and the trumpets of commonsense sound and resound in vain. Unhappily the walls of this citadel are very strong and do not fall. But within them rest men, who have steeled themselves against the Education that we seek in India and in 1962.

One of the dangers of the reverence I refer to is that, starting with religion, it comes in time, and sooner rather than later, to encroach upon and infect an entire way of education. To learn by rote, to use quotation as if it were argument, to cite authority for principle and precedent—all these are the consequence of placing upon a pedestal what should be on the floor. There is a tendency in our schools and colleges (and this is generally fostered), though there are splendid exceptions in all schools, some colleges and universities, there is a tendency to encourage this attitude of mind and behaviour. To judge an answer paper in literature, history and philosophy, sociology by its length, its volume of fact, its wealth of quotation and to miss the main point, which is the author's own contribution to the subject is sufficiently general in India today to be alarming. Has the student, having diligently collected his fact, thought round it? If so, what is the evidence? Is he merely reproducing what he has assimilated in the course of this reading and listening, or is he judging that reading as a scholar should? These are questions that require constantly to be asked. It does not fall to all of us to make original discoveries in metaphysics, logic or even literature.

But it surely falls to all of us to hold opinions and to make judgments that are not necessarily the transferred judgments of authority and pseudo-authority in such fields.

In my view it is better so thinking, so judging to make mistakes than unerringly, following the traditional path, to arrive at a conclusion that posterity and the stodgy present "know" to be true. As if knowing were ever final, as if Einsteins did not follow Newtons! For three parts of the business of the educational process is to travel, not hopefully necessarily, but vitally, with a constant responsiveness to stimuli, with sensibility and intellect bound together in that process of illumined integration in which idea, image and impression fuse into the streamlined pursuit of truth and excellence. Good tutors in India do not abound but they exist, and these are people who know it to be their function to get students to question what has been too easily accepted in the Humanities and the Sciences. Especially true is this of such a study as History in which the popular idea that thinking is not as necessary as it is in Science and Technology, is also (as always) the wrong idea. By what strange process of reasoning such a decision has been arrived at, and becomes, first, current and then rampant, till good students influenced by the topical prestige and marketability of science desert the history classroom for the laboratory, I cannot tell. Following the stream, good potential teachers of history are diverted from this vital species of discovery into the more popular and paying ways of science.

Lest I should be thought to be partisan between History, that is in decline in India in 1962, and Science that is moving steadily upwards to its appointed Everest, let me allay all fears. The only partisanship of which this paper and its author are guilty, are the partisanship for reason against superstition, for the lonely, unpopular thinker who refuses to be stampeded by waves of popular opinion and economic pressure into sacrificing the abiding truth that History, like Science, has to be exacting to be good. It may even be more exacting than Science because it is harder to verify. The student has, therefore, to be more cautious, not less so in his judgments. In dealing with the story of that which is not measurable or predictable, History has necessarily to draw upon imaginative experience. No doubt Science has also to do this and the stroke of genius that comes once a century or so is in reality the climax of a long procession of routine good work in which, somewhere, the flash of inspiration lies in nucleus awaiting the appropriate moment for discovery.

The second traditional value with which I would like to concern myself today is the value that places simplicity and austerity in living above comfort and a high standard of living. The whole treasury of the world's proverbs would appear to support the traditional Indian position on this. Cut your coat according to your cloth. We ants never borrow, we ants never lend. Waste not, want not. Kind hearts are more than coronets. Many a mickle makes a muckle. It is easier for a camel to pass through the eye of a needle than for a rich man to enter the Kingdom of Heaven. All this has a place somewhere in our thoughts as a corrective to the opposite that makes wealth a virtue and its pursuit, the business of the common man. Yet today in India what our Education most lacks is the ability to think with large, clear-eyed, feet-on-the-earth practicality.

Not long ago, I was in the Philippines to attend an Education Editors' Conference, and was introduced to the Community School of that country. Wherever I went I saw gaily coloured flower-pots, neatly gravelled paths and all the paraphernalia of daily routine entertainment. I was not surprised to see the schools so well-attended and the children so clean and tidy. For, surely, this is clear to men the world over today, as it is, has always been clear to women and children—a pretty school is the first step towards a good school. A school must attract children, not repel them by its hideousness. It is true that brick-and-mortar do not make a school, but no school can stand for long without brick and mortar. Yet with our traditional notions of austerity, the last thing that we seek to make a school is 'attractive'. A school is a building into which you send children to be rid of them. Stern, dark, uninviting, the inflexible laws of simplicity and austerity combine to make these places, that should be so well-remembered for joy and light and that sudden insight into what often felt to be, but is now seen to be places of cold instruction.

It is not surprising that this background of poverty informs the lives of our children for many years after they have left an elementary school. The slipshod is accepted; we can do no better. Dirt is accepted; we can do no better. It costs money to have shining floors and clean walls. I returned recently from a tour of colleges in a big city and can testify that every time I came across a good airy new modern building my heart leaped, my mind expanded to take in new ideas. For even we in the middle years can be educated by beauty, and beauty today appears to demand expenditure. Yet it is part of our insistent way of life to put money by, that should be spent. Savings campaigns may be patriotic from time to time, but there is by and large and in the long run, no virtue in either saving as a technique of living or in poverty as a way of thought and life. Such attitudes breed meanness, deprive the mind of its elasticity and run the risk of translating themselves into mean human relationships. They oust magnanimity, the generous impulse, the sustained habit of giving. I have observed for many years with unspoken distress, the acceptance in my country as a tradition, of the second-rate in preference to the first-rate even where we can afford the first-rate. And all this, because we are putting by for that proverbial rainy day that may perhaps never come, what should be spent today. If whole families over a subcontinent go on with this forever, we shall never have communities such as those of the Philippines that regard it as their bounden duty to support pretty schools. We shall never be able to shape public opinion to the wisdom of public and private expenditure on Education and the social appurtenances that make Education possible. A wise man once said, perhaps to offset the traditional omnibus of proverbs in favour of caution and providence: for every ten men who can save money, there is only one who can spend it wisely. For that is what economy means: it means wise expenditure, wise management, not the automatic impulse to hoard and then to pass barren gold or jewellery down to those who, to have diamonds in their ears, cast away the pearl of great price. This calls for a re-statement of priorities in national living so that those who live well, and not merely the meek shall inherit the land.

Abolish the tradition of reverence and replace it by the critical habit. Abolish the traditional notion that simplicity and austerity are good in themselves and replace them by the ability to spend and to live one's life with joy and vitality. We come to a third traditional value that modern India cannot afford to perpetuate, namely, the tradition of clouding in mystery what should be clearly understood and discussed in our classrooms and universities. I refer to the mysteries that surround sex. All this is bound up with our notion of what is right for society. Order, above all things. Women shall, therefore, be placed on a pedestal that was not too high for Sita but may be too high for her modern opposite. The virtues that we have venerated without sufficient examination—purity, chastity at any price, now require to be examined. Again, as a choice between these and their opposites— licentiousness, promiscuity, one would obviously prefer the Indian tradition. But the old virtues must not be taken for granted, since they close the mind to its natural impulses and duties. They must be re-examined. In themselves, these vaunted virtues may, indeed, stultify and reduce mental energy. They may keep a nation clouded, dark and weak. If science ever had a part to play in the life of the nation, surely this is it—that it should invade the private life of every citizen, male and female, and cast the light of candour, reason and forthright good sense upon what has been tucked away under a false sense of propriety and because we are—let's face it—afraid to see the implications of knowledge. But knowledge in this kind protects: it does not expose young girls and boys to the dangers that beset them with ignorance. In every college, of every university in the country, and even in the upper classes of Higher Secondary Schools, sex instruction is essential today. It is also essential in our present economy to explain and re-explain that large families are not divine gifts but prodigality that India cannot afford.

And this brings me to my last point. It is part of our inherited temper to ask to be analytic down to the smallest implication of an idea. We have no difficulty spelling out the theoretic implications of an idea, a proposition, a relationship. The educational problems of all nations today demand that this analytic faculty shall be exercised, and we might be presumed therefore to be a fortunately gifted people. The educational problems of old countries also, however, demand that they shall in their old age be adaptable countries that, having seen a problem, shall address themselves to its solution, first, with courage, then, with commonsense and, finally, with wholeheartedness.

With our analytic insight we often see to the heart of a problem. As we have not inherited any gift for swift or concerted executive action, and as we often enjoy the exercise of analysis, we do not go on to the business of constructive healing action with anything like the speed with which we resolve any analytic implications in our minds. Result: what is to be done is clear. What is in fact done either lags behind what should be done for months and years, or gets done in a rather haphazard blundering way. Concerted, responsible, timely, efficient action is still not a traditional way of life in India, and it is this, more than anything else, that accounts for the tardy solution of educational problems.

Having, for instance, accepted the theory of democracy we have seen to the heart of its implications in a country of over 400 million people. We have not been slow to see the need for compulsory primary education. In the more difficult reaches of secondary and university education, we are as yet feeling our way for the reason, primarily, that the implications of democracy are at conflict with our capacity to pay for it in ordinary economic-cum-educational terms and to decide what, with limited resources, we shall list as priorities.

The problem of numbers at university level is soluble on a national scale only if you have decided effectively to make secondary education a terminus for all those who are, for one reason or another, unfitted for higher education. This effective terminus—action at secondary level, we have not yet succeeded in taking 15 years from independence. The problem at university level has, therefore, squarely to be faced. The maintenance of standards demands that only those shall be admitted to universities even in a democracy who are fit for such an education. Not the wildest interpreters of democracy in 1962 in any part of the world would insist that, with limited resources for education, we could declare university education a fundamental right Even if these resources were not limited, I doubt if educationally such a case could be made out. And yet the argument swings backwards and forwards in the press and on public platforms in India. Admit them all. Admit third divisioners. Do not have entrance tests or vivas. Provide for everybody. And all this is urged in the name of democracy.

In these matters, with all her traditional values of persuasiveness, gentleness and tolerance, India has now to take a stand that is categorical, firm and rigid A university education, like a scholarship in 1962, has to be earned; it cannot be assumed to be a fundamental right. It has to be earned on merit exclusively. It is no more the prerogative of the rich and the noble, than it is of the pushing and the greedy. It is the reward of academic ability and industry. If we "accept" too much, we go in danger of acquiescing educationally and socially in what should be wiped out with the inflexible determination with which a democracy at war can work. And we are at war—educationally we are at war with ignorance, superstition and the dead-weight of centuries. We cannot afford to accept or tolerate these things. We need strong brooms to sweep away the cobwebs of the years. If, therefore, we seek to cling to the traditional value of a much-vaunted tolerance, let us not misinterpret it to mean the acceptance of what is without relevance or value for the times. We live in 1962. If we must accept the traditional values of patience and persuasiveness, let us also recognise that Time is our master and that it is vital here and now in 1962 to abandon the luxury of analysis for urgent executive action, that is practicable and implies collective and harmonious work in the immediate present. For, in the long run we are all dead. Too much tolerance in anything is bad; an intellect that retards action is also bad. Both must be re-formed.

I am sorry to have seemed so iconoclastic for one who is actually in favour of much that exists, and is certainly not against the essential values of harmony, persuasiveness and basic human tolerance. But there never was any national or individual progress that did not involve the rejection of what is outworn, and traditions that have outlived their usefulness are too obvious a liability for India to continue to bear. If, finally, you find it hard to forgive my unorthodoxy on national grounds, let me seek with a flippancy that is also a departure from our traditional value of solemnity, international forgiveness. You cannot have a Unescan omelette without breaking a few Indian eggs.

18

The Heart of the Matter*

The *NIE Journal* that makes its debut with this issue, is an amalgam of six periodicals brought out in earlier years by the National Council of Educational Research and Training. Dictated as much by the desire to integrate its content and reach, as to economise in the most rational sense of this abused word, the amalgamation of six periodicals presents a challenge that we are happy to accept. To pinpoint its public; to offer that public educational reading of varied facets consistent with uniform excellence; to serve as a forum for informed opinion without sacrificing principle to personality, fact to comment; consistently to stimulate thought on education in India, possibly by portraying thought and practice in other parts of the world—all these are our objectives. To the extent that we move towards and live up to them, we succeed.

The Journal will adopt a pivotal approach, that is, each issue will be based upon a single facet of contemporary Indian Education. On this, we hope to turn the searchlight of self-criticism, seeking always to move forward constructively. Necessarily, because the Journal is a professional medium, it will assume a certain level of professional information and knowledge, as well perhaps as educational values that we have a right to expect of those who practise Education in 1966.

---

*An inaugural editorial.

Our idiom will not, however, run to jargon or our readership constitute a freemasonary of experts. For it is our purpose to take in all those who, though possibly not immediately engaged in the common task in Education, are sufficiently involved in it marginally, to wish to recognise the signposts, and to learn how a modern educational compass works.

We will report news without comment though with evident selectivity. We will publish comment with the implication that we approve of it. And if, reading between the lines, our readers come in time to recognise a credo, a policy, a fighting premise in education, we shall not fail to defend it where necessary, or to propagate it in an enlightened national or international interest.

As the organ of the National Institute of Education, from which it takes its name, the Journal may, it seems, aspire without presumption to set, raise and emulate standards for India. The professional arm of the Union Ministry of Education could attempt no less.

Above all things, the NIE Journal will be a forum of informed judgment in Education. To its columns it welcomes writing in this kind of excellence, with which it may not necessarily agree. It surely is the mark of a liberal democracy that it recognises expressed differences of opinion as a necessary step to growth. Only by consistent, progressive analysis, exchange, interchange in the cross-fertilisation of disciplines, can a body of systematic educational knowledge grow, that we may dignify with the description of "Science". We stand as yet upon the threshold of things, groping our way through practice to theory and vice-versa, while the undiscovered ocean of knowledge seems to dash against the shores of our ignorance.

More practically, this issue is on teacher education to which in general it restricts itself. It begins with comment: it contains fact; it reports news; it records views; it criticises; it assesses experiments conducted; it publishes a summary of recommendations on teacher education by the Education Commission. To this last, we hope to bring in later issues critical appraisal by experts to which, we hope, our readers will react articulately. For we need in the common interest, to open a feature on Current Controversies, and few of them are either more current or more controversial than the education of our teachers.

This, at least, no one in India will dispute today: the teacher is the heart of the matter. You may build your schools of brick-and-mortar, of chromium and glass; you may debate the niceties of changing curricula and syllabuses, of textbooks and supplementary educational materials. You may grow old trying to force research to yield its reluctant conclusions or complicate further an already complicated framework of educational administration. All this is rendered superfluous unless you have educated your teacher, first, to know, and, then, to teach. Round this enormous twin problem, we compile our current issue, recognising that there are no easy solutions to the problems enunciated, that touch nearly five hundred million people in a subcontinent as old and as variegated as India. But hammer out solutions on how to educate our teachers we must, if we are to survive as a people. Thus, knowledge becomes commonsense. In the collective wisdom of the informed, with experience and analysis joining hands in training college and school classrooms, extension centres and advanced centres of research, we may find the bright beginnings of the distant answers we seek.

19

Literary Style and the Learning Experience

In his thought-provoking book on the process of education Jerome Bruner says:

> There has been little research done on the kind of concepts that a child brings to these subjects (i.e. Literature and History) although there is a wealth of observation and anecdote. Can one teach the structure and literary forms by presenting the child with a first part of the story and then having him complete it in the form of a comedy, a tragedy or a farce—without ever using such words? When, for example, does the idea of 'historical trend' develop and what are its precursors in the child? How does one make a child aware of literary style?

Happily for all of us, the world of learning cannot dogmatise on its answer to these searching questions. Whatever the precision of the answers that have so far been found to the learning of mathematics, science and logic in the most enlightened way, in language and literature we have no a priori judgments. We depend entirely on experience and the inductive method. We depend on verbal facility and the stimulus of an environment (that contains human beings, including a teacher or teachers and other children, and not excluding a library) to confer an insight into the need for style and its power to promote communication and knowledge.

It is probably one of the major sins of our secondary schools in India that they set little store at any time by style in the learning of a language and its literature. There have been teachers, and great teachers in other parts of the world (the one that occurs to me most insistently is a New Zealander, a woman, who taught Art and English to Maori children and then proclaimed in a small inspired book containing her experiences, that she saw her function as that 'of teaching style'.

In a country such as ours, burdened with the problem of content in all subject-fields, this may seem a perverse, or worse, an affected way of stressing the superfluous. It might well be argued that it is much more important to develop the reasoning habit among children at every stage than to stress what in any case comes to few children naturally, and what escapes most children who have missed the accent on beauty in their home environment.

What makes a child aware of literary style? To answer this, one ought to ask parallel questions such as: What makes a child aware of the golden light in a room she has just entered? What makes him aware of the difference between the gifted handling of a musical instrument and the skilled or semi-skilled performance that passes for playing the piano or the violin, the sitar or the veena? What makes the child see the differences between a poem and doggerel? When does the child weary of the lays of ancient Rome and exult strangely in 'My heart is like a singing bird' or a Walter de la Mare poem of which the best child anthologies in English are so wisely full, 'Silver' for instance?

Clearly, there are no easy answers to these questions because there are no 'average' children for the purpose of literary style. There is no normal, except in the purely statistical and meaningless sense of the word, reaction to beauty. The reaction that is worth having and noting and drawing inferences from is individual and unclassifiable. And this is where we must look for the nucleus of literary style. It cannot be acquired till it is perceived.

Can it be imitated? Yes, but this is probably the worst way to develop it as a learning experience. To parody seriously or for fun is not the best way to learn literature or to perceive and practise its finesse. The 'tumble' of inconsequential words that comes to many 'bright' children is not as frightening as many teachers of the old school feared. For most children, later gifted in the use of words to communicate and to bear testimony to their experience, begin with the 'tumble' of words, with a surfeit of adjectives. They have fallen in love with words for themselves.

Is this dangerous? It could be if it continued too long, for then, words would be used for their own sake, and not for the ideas they represent. This could well happen to children with an audio-sensitivity so sharp, that nothing was more important to them than a cascade of sound. For poetry, even at its simplest levels, is more than a cascade of meaningless sound; it is a cascade of sound containing something, that 'means' something, and not ratiocinative, but impressionistic.

But the problem is more complicated. The awareness of literary style is only one segment of an awareness of all beauty. The direction that this awareness takes will depend on a variety of things but chiefly on environmental factors and possibly hereditary sharpnesses and sensitivities, too. A child exposed in his earliest years to good music, good poetry reading, the fastidious use of language that means more than it states, the habit of conversation as opposed to that of talk, necessarily has a lead over a child to whom these things have, by an accident of either parentage or living conditions, been denied. Yet there was a Welsh miner called, Emlyn Williams (whose story he told in a play *The Corn is Green*) whose literary genius was revealed in a flash to an "inspired teacher" as he came to her out of the coal mine late one evening, fairly aching to proclaim the 'style' that lay undiscovered within him.

Is this then a latent strength that a wise teacher uncovers? It could be in some children, and these are twice-blessed, blessing those who teach and those who learn from them. But such people are rare. No teacher could afford to bank on jewels that the dark unfathomed caves of ocean bear.

It is much more sensible and rewarding to consider how to prepare children for this moment of awakening to beauty. It helps to have sensitive teachers, but we cannot depend entirely on the teacher-pupil relationship in large classes whose largeness makes discoveries such as Emlyn Williams very chancy. For children, not constantly exposed to the sound and sight of beauty (designedly I place sound and sight in that order, for literary style leans more heavily on the ear than on the eye) reading aloud in a resonant voice may be one of the techniques that yield the best results in time and depth. But how can we practise this in our unwieldy classes?

It cannot be done effectively in large classes. Indeed, one suspects that it can be done effectively only in the relaxing atmosphere of the home. Unless parents are capable of, and inclined to see the wisdom of this simple device regularly used, the child is in danger of losing what is essential to the cultivation of style in writing.

It is important to remember that there are no recipes, simple or complicated, for developing a literary style. This is an instance in which the learning experience can be evaluated only by considering and assessing a practical result. Matthew Arnold's criteria for good prose of lucidity, precision, rhythm and balance are probably at various levels all that is necessary to the writing of prose, though much that has been written since he died (including Papa Hemingway) would probably not have met his requirements. Nevertheless, it is a good rule in writing prose to insist on the absolute minimum of clarity. Unless the child knows what he wants to say, he will not be able to say it well. The adage that it is enough to think clearly to write clearly is unexceptionable. Style, unfortunately, involves more than clarity. Clear thinking may make clear, but not necessarily, beautiful writing. The element of style implies an element, often indefinable and elusive of beauty.

Apart from exposure to beauty early and consistently, how can this be taken and held captive for life?

There is no one way to secure it; there is no rule of thumb by which it can be taken and held captive. But it is probably true that the imagination and the intuition have constantly to be drawn upon, with challenges that may frequently tempt the child outside her own known experience to parallels and hypotheses such as: "If I were rich" or "If I were poor, then this is how I could think, what I would do" till the basic elements of tragedy and farce are stumbled upon, rather than scientifically discovered.

In conclusion, one must ask oneself whether the cultivation of a literary style is really as important as we seem to imply. This is not a matter of private judgment; it is a question of definition and implication. What do we seek when we seek style? I believe that in seeking style, we seek to develop the child's imagination and his capacity to testify to his experience, real and imaginative, with fidelity and high intensity. In working towards this end, we work towards the growth of powers that influence the total structure of a man's knowledge and power to communicate. The way one talks, writes and paints alters the content of what one says, writes and paints, the impact of one's thought upon those who draw their own stimulus from what they see, read and hear.

If it is not true, as Oscar Wilde believed, that "Books are neither good or bad; they are either well written or badly written" with the implication that style is all, it is true that style constitutes for many of us the only real insurance against being neglected by our fellows. To communicate is not enough. One has to communicate compellingly; and without the developed individualism that is equatable with literary style, the brightest child may remain inarticulate for life or so shoddily articulate that he is not heard or honoured. And for all human beings, this is a manifest tragedy.

20
Teacher*

Teacher by Sylvia Ashton-Warner, Bantam Matrix Edition, published in this edition, October 1964, originally published in 1963. 192 pages with several new plates.

First published in a hardback edition in 1963, *Teacher* now re-appears to our delight in paperback with a large number of new illustrative plates to make it, if that were possible, more vivid. Of its kind it is a classic: it says nothing that is not born of the passionate individual experience of an original teacher and philosopher: it is extraordinarily well-said and so has the capacity to continue to seem contemporary over the flying years.

A feature rather than a story in education, this book deals with the foundations of education in an elementary school in New Zealand where Maori children of five years and somewhat over, learn with white children. Mrs. Henderson (Sylvia Ashton-Warner in a thin disguise) seeks to let the encounter of cultures enrich both. She is, however, even more intent on the creativity of the climate that she can ensure for her "Little Ones" and particularly the Maori children to whom she is evidently dedicated. This leads her to believe and to test her conviction that all learning, to be real, natural and enduring, must be "organic", that is, "the way of growth where the

*A Review

strongest thing pushes up ahead of the less strong. In speaking of a child's mind I mean the strongest impulses push up, irrespective of whether or not they should, at a given time".

This, she applies to all aspects of teaching. As one would expect, she begins with Reading as a fundamental project and demonstrates how "First words must have intense meaning for a child. They must be part of his being." If this is so, the teaching of Reading must grow out of the familiar words and things of a culture-pattern, the way of life of a community, and this she applies to the Maori community of New Zealand that is sufficiently small and compact to be studied laboratory-wise. She argues that the children's Key Vocabulary centres round the two fundamental instincts of fear and sex and that, given the freedom to choose the words and the order of words that they learn, they learn easily, swiftly and for life.

From Reading, she moves to Writing, with the same sense of pursuing a course that must yield inevitably fruitful results.

"I never teach a child something and then get him to write about it. It would be an imposition in the way that it is in art. A child's writing is his own affair and is an exercise in integration that makes for better work. The more it means to him the more value it is to him."

The debit side of this arrangement, which is creatively irresistible, is that "Twelve (students) is the uttermost limit for one teacher. Eight is about the proper number." The results, of which the book contains many vivid and amusing examples, are remarkably good because evidently spontaneous. This, indeed, is one of Miss Ashton-Warner's obsessions: that educational discoveries, thinking and ideas must be spontaneous to be real, effective and susceptible of growth.

She has other and original things to say. The one that struck me as particularly worth considering was the need not to protect the child from sadness.

"Why is sorrow in such disgrace in infant-room reading fare? Kingsley's water-baby, Tom, had his despair. Alice in

Wonderland found herself in tight corners. David Copperfield had occasion enough to weep. Why then is a large part of infant-room reading so carefully and placidly two-dimensional? Is there any time of life when tears and trouble are not a part of living?"

As she proceeds to apply her ideas to all activity, whether reading or writing, nature study or numbers, painting or dancing, it is evident that Miss Ashton-Warner has done more than write a book; she has evolved a system of education as real as Neill's or Montessori's. This leads her rationally to her definition of a constantly disputed term. "Education fundamentally is the increase of the percentage of the conscious to the unconscious. It must be a developing idea. None of this is new, of course. It's the understood design of today's education."

A Preface by Sir Herbert Read will do something to induce the orthodox to read to the end of this revolutionary book. To the daring, anxious to see new ways of approaching, absorbing, and mastering knowledge, Sylvia Ashton-Warner is, however, good wine that needs no bush. As important for the way she says things, as for the content of what she urges, this small book will continue to be a classic, since it focuses on the unfolding of the child's mind in any part of the world at, any time.

21

Education in Three Stages

When I was ten, I said:
I want to know, yes, I must know
the reason why, I said;
And which and what and when,
and how and so, what then?
I want to know, I said.

They told me some of what
they thought that I must know—
The facts, the facts, the facts,
they said, of how we're born and grow,
and work and play.
And so I grew and worked and played
and thought I knew what
women need to know.
I passed for educated
at twenty.

And now I stand on the edge of life,
Still looking out, still asking questions
that neither 'they' nor pyramids of books
can answer. I no longer say:

I want to know, yes, I must know the reason why.
For no one knows except by tunnelling through
her blackest loneliness;
hacking, splintering, blasting, screeching through
the structured lie, geometric platitude,
the built-up whys and hows and so-what-thens
of the Establishment. If I must know, alone I go
to find what I may never know at fifty.

22
Educational Values

Whenever you go to an educational conference with colleagues in one or other phase or branch of education, you are re-vitalised by the exchange of experience. The chief merit of this exchange is that every professional recognises the need in the last resort to discuss fundamental educational values. Dodge these as we may, for it is never altogether easy or comfortable to discuss fundamental values, there is no way out. All educational discussion ultimately boils down to the values that you and others seasoned in education hold with the strength of a belief for life.

What does education mean to those who have practised it for a lifetime? I suspect that people do not generally formulate values when they go young into teaching or educational research. They know that they want to live a particular way, in the classroom in contact with the young, in and out of libraries where they can read to their mind's content. But an inclination to teach or to spend your life in places of learning is not quite the same thing as being able to enunciate educational values or being ready to do so. Now that my life is lived and it is more profitable to look back over the long corridor of experience than to look forward, I know that values cannot be formulated in a vacuum. You can do so with wisdom and some degree of certainty only with a background of intensive experience. This is the only respect in which the old who have lived their lives with sense and humility, are better equipped to teach than the young. And so when people who have spent the greater part of their working lives educating others and (more important) themselves, meet to compare notes and exchange experience, something like a system of values emerges.

What are these values about? In the first place, some part of us, and possibly a more important part than we are willing to allow in our environmental times, is inherited. Without our ancestors, some people think with reason, we are nothing. We have imbibed from the air about us as we have grown up, a composite of biases and prejudices, that we rarely clarify or evaluate, towards learning and life. When these attitudes crystallise into a tradition with geographic and cultural boundaries, we tend to think of them as constituting a national tradition, our tradition.

The tradition in India was certainly one of dedication to scholarship, respect for learning and the symbol of learning, the Teacher; humility in the pupil, frequently blind obedience on his side. What your teacher told you to do, you did. Humility could go no further. You proved your dedication by cooking your guru's food, washing his clothes, living life as he laid down that it should be lived, away from your parents and committed to your guru's clemency or his rigidity. You set yourself to imitate what you revered. Reverence dictated obedience.

This is the Indian tradition, and that there was much good in it, we would probably not deny even in our own permissive times. The student who does not approach learning with humility, falls by the wayside. The student who does not seek learning for its own sake at some time, is, to put it mildly, not ideal. The attachment to the man through whom truth is made available is manifestly noble. There was no quid pro quo between teacher and taught. The one gave, the other took without thought of commercial gain. To conserve learning and interpret it—this was more important in ancient India than to discover new things.

There is, however, a fundamentally different tradition that came to us much later though it, too, sprang of an ancient people, the Greeks. Socrates, who stands for this different tradition, will not be remembered for his humility, though he will be remembered for his love of truth. He will not be remembered for his obedience to a settled tradition of learning, though he will be remembered for his unworldliness and his abiding contempt for riches and the epicurean life. He will not be remembered for his massive scholarship, but he will be remembered for his questioning mind. Indeed, if we wish to spotlight the Socratic view of the meaning of education, we find it in his dictum that "the unexamined life is not worth living".

To his judges, defending his way of life when he was on trial for corrupting the youth of Athens, Socrates is reported as saying: "Wherefore O judges, be of good cheer about death, and know of a certainty that to a good man, no evil can happen either in life or after death. Still...I have a favour to ask. When my sons are grown up, I would ask you, O my friends, to punish them, and I would have you trouble them as I have troubled you. if they seem to care about riches or anything more than about their virtue; or if they pretend to be something when they are really nothing, then reprove them, as I have reproved you, for not caring about that for which they ought to care, and thinking that they are something when they are really nothing. And if you do this, both my sons and I will have received justice at your hands"

To those, again, who urged that he should meet his critics half-way, Socrates is reported to have said:

"Someone will say: 'Yes, Socrates, but cannot you hold your tongue and then you may go into a foreign city, and no one will interfere with you?' Now I have great difficulty in making you understand my answer to this. For if I tell you that to do as you say would be a disobedience to the God, and therefore, that I cannot hold my tongue, you will not believe that I am serious; and if I say again that daily to discourse about virtue, and of those other things, about which you hear me examining myself and others, is the greatest good of man and that the unexamined life is not worth living, you are still less likely to believe me. Yet I say what is true, although a thing of which it is hard for me to persuade you".

If we compare the traditional attitude to scholarship in India with the Socratic view we see that there are elements both of likeness and unlikeness. Both opt for knowing as a value to be preferred to acquiring wealth or exercising power over others. Knowledge is paramount in both systems. Sumptuousness is despised both by our ancient gurus and by Socrates. 'Mind is best', both systems seem to be saying, 'I will seize mind, forgo the rest'.

Undoubtedly, though the *chela* in India was required to place implicit faith in his guru while he was a pupil, he, too, had the chance later to examine other systems and life and to compare what he had learnt with what others taught, and with what life itself taught. You will recall that Hermann Hesse's Siddhartha chooses to abandon the Brahman's way of life that he has learned from his fathers, in order to become a samana or wandering ascetic, and to find things out for himself. His friend, Govinda, who is much more typical, follows others stronger and wiser than himself. He has the docility of the traditional Indian pupil. He rarely strides out of a tradition as Siddhartha does. When both young men meet Gautam Buddha, Govinda is easily persuaded that this is the teacher from whom he can learn most. Not so Siddhartha who, though he has a genuine respect for the Buddha, plunges into a life of his own, not always creditable. But he does recognise that the Buddha has left him with his identity. We will return to this question of thinking human identity later in this talk.

As Hesse portrays Siddhartha, the young man stands somewhere between the Indian and the Socratic traditions. The function of the Socratic way is to, question, It is to decline to accept what you have not examined. It is of its essence an attitude of criticism to learning and life. It is ruthless in the demands that it makes both of students and of teachers. All this is done with great amiability, with a kind of sweet irony but also with an inflexible persistence. Socrates is never openly rude, merely insistent in rejecting what does not satisfy his analytic mind Ordinarily classed as a sophist, Socrates is in fact a sophist with a marked difference. Since he chooses to die when, by a compromise or by silence, he could continue to live, we may be sure that there is nothing bogus about him. At his trial, he defends the fundamental values that all free men have defended since this first great martyr to independent thinking drank his cup of hemlock.

I may seem to oversimplify the two attitudes to education when I describe the one as fundamentally critical and enquiring, and the other as reverential and conserving, that concentrates on interpreting stored wisdom. But these are the two extreme attitudes to learning and life. Most of us use now the one, now the other in learning and living. We are not so sure of ourselves that we can claim, as Socrates did, not to accept what we have not examined for ourselves. We take some things on trust. Yet we often feel the need to re-examine the supposedly incontestable wisdom of the ages. Of course, we would be guilty of all manner of absurdity if we over-stressed the one attitude or the other in the business of living. When I hear young people stress the need for originality and the superior value of originality over factual verified information, I am tempted to ask: "Original about what?" Originality must clearly base itself on knowledge of some kind. You have to know something to be able to think about it originally. Then, there is the opposite extreme that epitomises itself in the cliche that "a man's knowledge is as good as his information", another nonsense, since it rules out a priori knowledge, the intuitive recognition of basic and irresistible truths.

Now, let us go back to the business of modern educational discussion with which I started. When we confer today, it is on a much more mundane level than Socrates or the Buddha.

It is on, for instance, what education is for in the modern world. But if we think that because centuries divide us from Socrates, we can dispense with his values, we are mistaken. When he said that education was to enable him to get at the truth and to cultivate virtue, he was putting it in the all embracing way that the Greeks—all power to them—were given to using. When we say that education is for life in society, are we saying something basically different?

Socrates was not exclusively concerned with the thinking process. He was concerned with the application of clear thought to the problems of living, of man in society. When he spoke of the unexamined life as not being worth living, it was precisely about social man that he was talking. He was charged in fact with a social crime, that of corrupting the youth of Athens, and he believed that it would not be worth living if he did not continue to examine life aloud, for others within his society to hear. It is a point that the other great human landmarks in the story of education are all concerned, as was Socrates, both with a man's duty to himself and to his society. Comenius, the Czech; Rousseau, the Frenchman; Pestalozzi the Swiss; Froebel, the German; Dewey, the American are all concerned in their various ways with the development of human personality, with rights and wrongs, within the orbit of human society as they know it at different times, in different places. No one is basically concerned with man in isolation, on an island of his own.

When, therefore, we say in India today that we educate boys and girls, men and women, to enable them to live their lives to capacity within the society into which they happen to have been born, we are not basically in conflict with Socrates, though we are more circumscribed than he was. In a country as far-flung as India, we must necessarily have educational priorities dictated by the needs of particular people in a particular environment, and this includes a composite of circumstances—language, history, cultural attitudes, the physical potential of the area, the implications for life and work within it, the investment available for it. We argue that this is generally where most students are going to live their lives, and that to enunciate priorities where resources are so limited is sensible.

So far so good. But the manner in which education is given determines whether the values underlying it are sound or not. If the student educated on the principle that he is being educated for life within a specific geographic and cultural area, is educated to think only cf his area, its needs and his obligations to it, I would say that the values underlying his instruction are not sound. If, on the other hand, he is educated primarily for life in that area, but with an openness to other kinds of society, other ways of thinking and behaving and with a constant flexibility of movement backwards and forwards in time, so that he sees the connection between a fact and the concept underlying related facts in time, the concrete detail and the abstract universal that explains facts and details, the values on which he is raised are sound. The teacher's function is, by illuminating concepts, to enable the student to learn for himself.

When we ask a question that is asked ad nauseam in India today: Education for what? this may be analysed further into:

(i) Is education for being? or

(ii) It it for doing?

In the short term, and because life is finite, education should enable you to do. But doing is always a half-way house to being. Doing enables us to be. It shapes us, forms mind and body, a way of thought, work and play, attitudes to people, attitudes to ourselves in living and dying. Ironically, it is only through doing that we obtain the self-knowledge that is intrinsic to the business of education. There is no contradiction between doing and being, the one makes the other possible. They stress a man's duty to himself and his duty to society, what he owes himself as an individual and what is due from him as a citizen. Where conflict arises between these imperatives as it did for Antigone, it is for the individual to decide what his/her ultimate value is, and to act in accordance with it.

If you agree with my argument that the business of education is to equip the student to do his own learning and living, it will be clear that there is no time limit, short of life itself, to education. It does not begin at 6, when you start going to school and end at 21, when you start going to work. It begins the moment you can feel and think, and does not end till you cease to feel and think. It is coterminous with life. Once you see education as coincidental with life, you shake off the old and current superstitions about it: that it is dull; that it is theoretic and academic, a hothouse plant bred in the atmosphere of a classroom, that is irrelevant to the business of living. There is in fact no experience, not even a sensation that does not educate. Anything at all that contributes to a knowledge of life is education. Some part of this is more formalised than other parts of it, and we have therefore evolved, as an educational shorthand, such phrases: "Where were you educated?" But that is a matter of words and the limitations that words impose on thought and meaning. The truth about educational values is, as Socrates, said: for the educated, the unexamined life is not worth living,

I said earlier that I would return to the question of thinking human identity. Listen now to what Hannah Arendt, a modern philosopher, has to say on this crucial concept that goes back to Socrates. "Everybody may come to shun that intercourse with oneself whose feasibility and importance Socrates first discovered. Thinking accompanies life and is itself the de-materialised quintessence of being alive; and since life is a process, its quintessence can lie only in the actual thinking process, and not in any solid results or specific thoughts. A life without thinking is quite possible; such a life fails to develop its own essence—not merely is it meaningless, but it is not fully alive. Unthinking men are like sleepwalkers".

Equate education with life—and life means all of it from birth to death—and you have seen education the right side up. Indeed, you have penetrated to the most important of all educational values.

Teaching and Learning

A sculpture entitled First Steps by Mile. Bricard fascinates all mothers and would be teachers. In it a very small child just learning to walk, totters towards its mother who, with arms outstretched, is a guarantee of progress with safety. The two figures, the one trying to do, the other trying to make doing possible, are united in a composition so much more eloquent than the material invested in it, that it has become a symbol of the standard relationship of mother—and—child, teacher—and—pupil for all time. Such a stereotype probably accounts for the general belief that mothers are the first instinctive teachers, when, that is, they do not deliberately abdicate the right by delegating it to a nurse. The two elements that underlie First Steps are love and the instinctive communication, through love, of knowledge.

And yet, there is good reason to suppose that mothers are not, after all, the best teachers. The sort of love that mothers have for their children is as often stultifying as stimulating. A mother is often not a good teacher for one of two widely different reasons. Either she is too ambitious for her child, drives him or her with a passion for self-realisation that can do the child no good and may well harm it for life; or, alternatively, a mother is over-protective, that is, not stimulating enough. Though her instincts clearly proceed from love, they are not necessarily the best equipment for a teacher.

One reason, though not the only reason, why the history of education is so permanently interesting is that for centuries men have either asked the wrong questions of themselves and others, or have asked questions with the wrong emphasis. With the advantage of hindsight, we can now look back and see through what labyrinths we have reached our present still-imperfect knowledge of what we are really seeking. Through the centuries, teaching and learning have been tied together almost inextricably. Sometimes men have accorded learning the importance it deserves but, more generally, it is teaching with which they have been concerned, as if no learning were possible without teaching, and as if the whole business of education centred on the teacher. Broad-minded, large-hearted men throughout have, indeed, sought to benefit the child, but the child has not always been the centre of education. The discoverers seem more often to have been bent on observing the process of teaching, than the process of learning. And till the advent of Rousseau, even the child was an after-thought. All attention was concentrated on how to be a good teacher for any age-group.

Incidentally, while making their discoveries educationists have clearly been concerned with the ends of education. They have asked themselves whether the end is knowledge or morality or character. Whether it is more important to make good minds in individuals or good social beings for society. What is the purpose of educating? And does education make us better people? But through all these questions, we rarely seem to pinpoint the learner. Rather, it is the process through which learning is communicated and the ends for which it is achieved that seem to bother men.

Thus, observe Comenius, the Czech. In his Pansopia or 'Universal Wisdom', Comenius included three main ideas: first, an encyclopedia of universal learning; second, the idea of promoting scientific discovery by establishing a college in which all the necessary conditions of scientific discovery would be available; and third, the recognition that teaching and research are inter-dependent. Through these three steps Comenius came to the problem of a new method (mark that word, that will repeat itself through our exploration) of instruction, that every individual shall be able to avail himself to the limit of his capacity, of the benefits of knowledge in all fields of learning.

Then came Rousseau, sometimes referred to as the "Copernicus of Modern Civilisation," with a truly valuable discovery. Here he is:

"We never know", he says, "how to put ourselves in the place of children; we do not enter into their ideas, but we ascribe to them our own."

Rousseau made the discovery from which we are now profiting, that teaching and training do not consist in inculcating ideas, but in furnishing the child with the opportunity to function at each stage in a way that is natural to that stage of development. Listen, again, to Rousseau in his own inimitable voice: "We do not know childhood. Acting on the false ideas we have of it, the further we go, the further we wander from the right path. Those who are wise are attached to what is important for men to know without considering what children are able to apprehend. They are always looking for the man in the child, without thinking of what he was before he became a man. This is the study upon which I am most intent, to the end that, though my method may be chimerical and false, profit may always be derived from my observations. I may have a very poor conception of what ought to be done, but I think I have a correct view of the subject on which we are to operate. Begin, then, by studying your pupils more thoroughly for it is very certain that you do not know them".

With that push in the right direction, we get something like a theory of development in which the child or learner passes through progressive stages Words like 'animal', 'self-consciousness', 'memory', 'connected memories', 'rationality', 'puberty', 'sex' all fall into approximately their modern places, from which Freud clearly benefited. But the emphasis is still not all that can be desired, for we are still pursuing a method of teaching. And though observation is an inherent part of this discovery of method, it is teaching that we are seeking to perfect, not intrinsically learning.

There follows Pestalozzi who derived much from Rousseau, and particularly his emphasis on sense-experience. Pestalozzi profited from his own deprived social background. He saw the school as a second heme, and was enormously enthused when a peasant who saw a Pestalozzi school for the first time, ingenuously exclaimed:

"Why, this is not a school, but a family!" "Ha!" cried the triumphant Pestalozzi: "That is the greatest praise that you can give me." He then proceeded to outline his theory, which is that the teacher should aim rather at increasing the powers of his pupil than at increasing his knowledge. Now, this, though it may seem elementary today, was a great advance. Intensify the capacity of the learner to learn through teaching, and that is more valuable than any information that you can stuff into him. Learning, says Pestalozzi, should always be a spontaneous process, a result of free activity, a living and original product. And with extraordinary wisdom, he looks back and evaluates his own contribution to education. "I find", he says, "that I have fixed the highest supreme principle of instruction in the recognition of sense-impression as the absolute foundation of all knowledge".

Perhaps we ought to pause here to consider his self-evaluation. Comenius, before Pestalozzi, had insisted on the value of pictures in educating small children. Pestalozzi, by contrast, insists on the objects that precede pictures. A child must be educated through sense-perception of the thing-in-itself. The mind is not passive or merely receptive; it is implicated in sense-experience. We realise the value of this discovery much later when Anne Sullivan is trying to teach the blind-and-deaf Helen Keller. The child is extremely intelligent and vigorous, and Anne has discovered how to teach her the deaf language. So words accumulate in Helen's hungry hand and mind. But the obstreperous little girl has expended her energy in amassing a word vocabulary that has no meaning, for she cannot see the objects to which the words apply. Then Anne, possibly on her own, but certainly applying the wisdom of Pestalozzi, finds the object to which an important word applies. She finds meaning, she finds the concept when she puts Helen's learning hand under running water from a water-pump in the garden. Helen learns to connect the word 'water' with the object that is fluid and life-giving. And so she can now use 'water' to signify both the literal and the figurative things to which we apply the word in life.

Reacting to Rousseau, men got the notion that all learning should be made pleasant and easy. It must involve no hardship, no effort. All learning must be made play, 'soft pedagogy' as we call it today. But then came the stern German Herbart with the stiffening that this easy notion required. Herbart insisted on instruction to cultivate clearness, definiteness, continuity of thought. All education, he said, depends alone on instruction, and ideas and knowledge are the source of good feeling and virtue. His aim was morality in the large sense in which Socrates desired it. Character was the aim of education, but knowledge, said Herbart, builds and produces a mind. Knowledge is no longer just a mental element—it makes the mind possible: It is through knowledge and instruction that such a thing as the mind develops.

This was amplified further by the German Froebel. All real development, Froebel taught, stems from self-activity, constructive activity, that harmonises spontaneity and social control. Knowledge is not an end, but functions in relation to the activities of the organism. And finally, for our purpose, came the American Dewey with other important considerations that are still on the anvil and have been, as they should be, as fervently disputed as proclaimed. Education, Dewey says, is a process, not a product. Infancy, youth and adult life all stand on the same educative level, in the sense that what is really learned at any and every stage of experience constitutes the value of that experience. We hear new words and phrases—"process of living", "socialisation", "instrumentalism", "pragmatism". And the stress is on man as a social being, though this does not preclude the development of the individual.

The result of over-emphasising method through centuries of analysis is the tendency to equate education with methodology, and this explains the setting up of thousands of teacher-education institutes and colleges that are in effect attempts to provide expertise in how to teach as if the manner of communication were all. It is dangerous to assume that content in what is taught is subordinate to the manner of its communication. It should never be a question of either content or method. It has to be both, and it would be best of all not to separate them, for the method flows from the content, as surely as style flows from the man. The most ingenious methodologist cannot teach what he does not deeply and extensively know. A non-knowledgeable teacher is a contradiction in terms, A knowledgeable teacher, who has not discovered the best way to communicate what he knows, can possibly be taught to do this. The non-knowledgeable teacher has to go back to learn his subject. And this is really much more fundamental as the world's knowledge multiplies, than learning the skill of communication.

If, then, the right emphasis for us today is not on how to teach, and the teacher is no longer the heart of the process of knowing and living, what is his pure function? Can we dispense with him or her? Where is he/she most needed?

These are relevant questions for our times. We cannot altogether dispense with the teacher, and I am talking of the everyday teacher, not the prophet, because learning, which is the heart of education, must proceed from somewhere, and the teacher can simplify the process for us. He is not the sole source of learning, as so many of our forefathers thought, but he is possibly the most important single medium through which the learner learns. At the more elementary stages of learning, the teacher qua teacher is more necessary than he/she is later when the learner has acquired the skills of learning for himself. But the proviso that makes the teacher useful at any stage of education is that he will always himself be a learner. There is no stage for the teacher at which his learning is done, and he can lie back and begin to teach without more sustained learning. For teaching is the other face of learning. It confirms and promotes learning in the teacher. It is part of the developmental process of mind that Rousseau and, later, Herbart were to hammer home. Education, as Dewey insists, is convertible with life. Therefore, educators must never cease to learn, for only when they can assist the learning process, have they earned the special value that we have come to place on them.

Tagore expressed this as well as it can be, when he said: "A teacher can never truly teach unless he is still learning himself. A lamp can never light another lamp unless it continues to burn its own flame. The teacher who has come to the end of his subject, who has no living traffic with his own knowledge, but merely repeats his lesson to his students can only load their minds. He cannot quicken them. Truth not only must inform, but also must inspire. If the inspiration dies out, and the information only accumulates, then truth loses its infinity. The greater part of our learning in the schools has been waste, because for most of our teachers their subjects are like dead specimens of once living things, with which they have a learned acquaintance, but no communication of life and love."

Where a child is deprived, as Helen Keller was, a teacher would seem to me to be indispensable and the teacher's obligations are then total. Nothing but making the child in the initial stages depend on his teacher, will solve the problem of physical or mental deprivation. For normal children and, at later stages of formal education, the teacher's function is to teach his student how to learn for himself. This must be done conceptually as Pestalozzi taught, and as Herbart confirmed. Once develop in a student the ability to acquire not facts but concepts, water, the thing-in-itself and not merely the word 'water', and the teacher's job is done. As soon as a teacher's students are independent of him as a result of the teaching they have received from him, the teacher is freed to devote himself to those who really need him. In a word, the test of good teaching is the confidence that a teacher gives his students that they can do their own learning. The quicker and more permanently this confidence is communicated, the better the teacher.

The discoveries about teaching and learning have gone on through the centuries—yet we feel that we are still only on the threshold of educational wisdom. This is so partly because we know so little as yet about the human brain, its capacities, its scope for development. It is so partly because man is still so much in a developmental social stage that the future of the race seems imaginatively to unfold before him in almost limitless possibilities of experiment and discovery as a social being. But with the tools that we have, we should go far. Exploration has taught us that the learner, not the teacher, is the heart of the matter, that there are as many ways of teaching as there are ways of learning. Where teaching has destroyed itself by inertia or desiccation, there are other ways for students to learn that we may use in the 20th century. Exploration goes on through such modern thinking as this:

> "There has been little research done on the kind of concepts that a child brings to literature and history although there is a wealth of observation and anecdote. Can one teach the structure of literary forms by presenting the child with a first part of the story and then having him complete it in the form of a comedy, a tragedy or a farce, without ever using such words?" That was Jerome Bruner in *The Process of Education.*
>
> And, finally, consider this:
>
> "Education fundamentally is the increase of the percentage of the conscious to the unconscious. It must be a developing idea. None of this is new of course. It's the understood design of today's education". That was Sylvia Ashton-Warner in her book *Teacher,* and underlying her 20th century words, are echoes of Rousseau and Freud.

New Directions

Our two previous explorations have brought us to this point: that the learning process, which is the heart of education, begins at birth and ends only with the cessation of life.

This proposition sums up the challenge to education in the 20th century. In 1978, no one enlightened can doubt that few things in the world liberate men as education does. When once a people or a nation begins to think, it is impossible to stop it. In 20th century terms, this means that for developing societies such as ours, education is the single most potent instrument of change that man knows and that, with it, though he certainly cannot solve all his problems, he can create a climate in which it becomes possible for him to state them and to seek solutions to them with a reasonable hope of success.

The first of many challenges that the 20th century has offered education is that everyone, not just an elite, but everyone in every part of the world, must have the chance to be educated. The implications are clear. If we were to depend solely on teachers to educate all the learners in the world, we would be confronted with a shortage of teachers, for the education of teachers is not an easy or economic matter; and the production of good teachers is a much more difficult process than many planners suppose. If, therefore, we are short of teachers and crucially short of good teachers for our 20th century goals in learning, from whom or what will the learner learn?

Necessity, they say, is the mother of invention, and the 20th century revolutions in science and technology may well have been responses to democratic and qualitative compulsions. The teacher has always more or less used a book or books to assist him. The textbook and the supplementary reader, to say nothing of whole libraries of general books, used to be regarded as teaching aids, when the teacher was the centre of the educational process. Since he ceased to be that, we have found in textbooks produced by the million in a very short time, substitutes for him. It is still probably true that a good teacher is the best single source of learning, provided, that is, he is like Tagore's teacher, a learner in himself. Only good teachers can write good textbooks, but good textbooks are not written exclusively by good teachers. They are an example of that inter-disciplinary team-work that is characteristic of our century's learning. They imply the work of the subject specialist, specialists in allied fields, the methodologist and the editor to communicate effectively, the artist, where the book is illustrated, the evaluator, and so on.

The good textbook has certain evident advantages as a source of learning over the good teacher, and it has immense advantages over average teachers. The book is portable and so is always with us, whereas the teacher, being himself a human being, is not physically at our disposal at all times. If the textbook is well constructed, it answers questions; it has supplementary exercises, specific answers to specific questions, explanations of method, a glossary, and it frequently supplies background material in a manner so inspired and memorable that the textbook becomes in its own right a classic. Such a textbook was Warde Fowler's *City State* that was just as easy to remember as any celebrated work of fiction or poetry. Of how many teachers can it be said that they are classics in their field?

How shall we produce really outstanding textbooks? As far back as Comenius, we learnt that teaching and research must go together as a source of learning. Research has done more in our century than ever before to ask the right questions. One of these is: how can the foundations of any subject be taught to anybody at any time? For we are now sure that they can be taught is some form. The point is to discover the form. If the function of the teacher is what we found it to be in our second exploration, that is, to teach the student how to learn for himself, then in essence learning is initially not a skill, but a general idea or concept which can be used as a basis for recognising subsequent problems, as special cases of the idea originally mastered. This is what we mean by "conceptual" learning.

Among other important things that modern research is anxious to discover is how to make intuitive thinking more general than it is. It is clear that some students leap at the truth that their own teachers have had to grope to find. Intuitive thinking characteristically does not advance in careful well-defined steps. The thinker arrives at an answer which may be right or wrong with little, if any, awareness of the process by which he reached it. He can rarely provide an adequate account of how he obtained his answer and he may be unaware of just what aspects of the situation he was responding to. Usually, intuitive thinking rests on our being familiar with the area of knowledge involved, and this makes it possible for the thinker to leap about, skipping steps and using short cuts in a way that requires later checking. Jerome Bruner tells us that at the University of Buffalo, there is a collection of successive drafts of poems written by leading contemporary poets. One is struck in examining them, he says, by the immediate sense one gets of the tightness of a revision a poet has made, but it is often difficult or impossible to say why the revision is better than the original. And this may be as difficult for the poet to tell as for the reader.

Research has also taught us how to transform descriptive learning material into analytic problem-solving material. There is a striking difference between a person who thinks that the task before him represents a problem to be solved, and one who feels that he is controlled by random forces. To solve or to try to solve problems comes natural to thinking men. Witness the popularity of detective fiction where the dominant problems are who committed the crime and how? The whole process of self-conscious reflectiveness has been the subject of 20th century research with discovery-in-learning for a goal. How do we teach something to a child, arrange his environment so that he can learn something with the assurance that he will use the material he has learned appropriately in varied situations?

The superior and the older child need teaching less than the average and the younger child. But there is a stage—I would say anything between 15 and 20 years in which students do not need teaching. Experiments conducted in many parts of the world have convinced me that the use, for instance, of the Library Seminar, is a more effective way to understand literature and possibly the social studies than the lecture method that we still use in most of our universities. The library/seminar is an experiment in learning by a group of able, homogeneous students who learn by mastering and analysing a book chosen for its capacity to stimulate deep thinking at an abstract level. The only assistance that the students have other than a library is an older learner, a teacher who continues to learn. For teaching is, of course, a superb way to learn. There is a beautiful story told about a distinguished teacher of Physics. He reports that he tried to introduce the Quantum Theory to an advanced class. "I went through it once and looked up only to find the class full of blank faces, they had obviously not understood. I went through it a second time and they still did not understand it. And so I went through it a third time and that time I understood it." So, in a library seminar the book wisely chosen is analysed, discussed by able students among themselves in the presence of a learning-teacher who intervenes only when absolutely necessary. The students collectively learn round and through a book. Research with feedback helps to make outstanding textbooks.

In the learning society that the 20th century has become by its eighth decade, we do not need children who merely learn to walk and talk and read and write. Rather, we need children, adolescents and adults, each of whom is learning at an appropriate pace and with all the special advantages and disadvantages peculiar to his own age. The times we live in are exactingly democratic. They are also exactingly qualitative: nothing but excellence will do. Numbers are now involved that have never been considered for education in earlier centuries. And that is why technology has been called in, in a big way, to help men out with what they cannot do physically for themselves.

"A good home", says Robert Hulchins, "is one in which there are books, conversation, a respect for learning. The lack of ability among the poor that is everywhere lamented is a consequence of the conditions under which they are brought up. The school cannot compete with or remedy these conditions. All it can do is to palliate its worst effects".

This statement is worth examining for at least two reasons. First, it implies that in the short period for which schools have children, they cannot do enough to offset the disadvantages of barren homes. Where the home can help the school, it must. But the home can, in millions of cases, not help at all. We have therefore to find a way to deal with the disadvantaged home and only technology can help us out. Second, we recognise that the good home is not necessarily the affluent home; it is a home in which there is access to learning, to books, conversation in which, by 20th century standards, children can begin to examine life.

The object of technology is increased efficiency or a larger quantity at a cheaper rate. The plastic cup, not Cellini's goblet, is the symbol of a scientific and technological age. The plastic cup will hold liquid as well as, if not as long as, Cellini's masterpiece. And it can do so, while it lasts, for millions of previously cupless people round the world. But though efficiency is a legitimate aim for those engaged in transmitting information, it can provide an answer only to questions with a single answer. When the questions have many answers, or we are trying to learn something other than the answers, such as appreciation, principles, understanding, the machine is up against highly recalcitrant material. With technology, you can pinpoint the facts of the philosopher's life. But you cannot find the right answer to the question of what he means to the history of man.

Sir Eric Ashby, who gave Ghana her first blueprint for national education, says:

"Technology is inseparable from a money economy. It assumes a competitive society. It assumes obedience to the clock. It assumes that the individual can detach himself from the matrix of his family and village and exercise his individuality. All these assumptions are anathema to traditional African society." And we may add that traditional Indian society hasn't taken kindly to them, either.

Nevertheless, think what technology can achieve that was never possible before our century's technological revolution. Programmed learning, that we use in correspondence literature, can dispense with a large number of teachers and also with the expensive brick-and-mortar of our traditional schools and colleges. It can enable the student to proceed in learning at his own pace. Motion pictures and television can present the lectures of good teachers in place of the lectures of poor teachers. Radio can bring Laurence Olivier's and John Gielgud's speech to the understanding by millions of Shakespeare. Reproduction of any process, artistic or scientific, can be brought into the classroom. Thus, an experiment performed under ideal conditions in a laboratory can be filmed and watched by successive thousands, replacing one performed under imperfect conditions, that can be seen by only a dozen students at a time. The classroom itself can be abolished if we choose, and all teaching and learning can be carried on individually in the home or in small groups wherever they find it convenient to assemble. Microfilm and computers eliminate space and time operations which would otherwise demand years of travel or calculation. Thus, if the state steps in with technology to relieve the poor home of its disadvantages, the poor child can learn at par with his affluent counterpart. We can now conquer the barrenness of poverty.

As against this, we do have to remember that technology needs to be controlled. The net result of replacing the human teacher by the machine is that we will tend perhaps to diminish the attention given to reasoning and judgment. We will reduce discussion, because machines do not talk back as human beings do. We are in danger of having mass education with all its weaknesses and against these we have to be forearmed.

But with control, with imagination, intellect, with the advantage of being able to use the best minds and talents in chosen fields for learning, we can have successful Open Universities that use the mass media in the service of all men and all women, in the learning process. The teacher is indeed built into such a system, but the teacher is used with supreme economy. Only outstanding teachers are inducted into the system to prove, while it is on trial, that it can serve large numbers of varied people just as well as, or possibly better than the expensive brick-and-mortar colleges of traditional instruction. Democracy has therefore triumphed through technology, and excellence in some kinds has been achieved.

Does technology alter the fundamental educational values with which we started our exploration? Not at all. It is plainly an aid, a method of making values known and available to those who seek them. It is a means to an end, not in itself an end. If Socrates could have lived in our times and observed the problems that beset us, it is more than likely that he would have approved of the application of technology to the solution of problems, but only after asking all the awkward questions that intellectual critics of technology have asked, and continue to ask to ensure that we never sacrifice intellectual content to speed and mechanical efficiency in learning. Thinking is still at the heart of the learning process, and the learning process is much more than a way to master facts. But without the facts there is no data for knowledge. Without knowledge there is no mind. Without the mind, there is no agency through which man will progressively master his environment and study the imponderables. Technology does not alter the central problem; it merely makes it easier to solve. Centuries after Socrates drank his cup of hemlock, we say, using all the media evolved with the aid of technology, exactly what he said: "The unexamined life is not worth living".

23

What to do with Public Schools

Let me say right away that I have the highest admiration, within their idiom, for all that the Public Schools of India have done in the past and are possibly doing at present. They have created a style in education of their own, accepting a legacy from Britain and adapting it to Indian circumstances, in so far as this is possible. They have created, maintained and, I truly believe, sought to promote standards of excellence in education, in teaching and learning. They have honoured their precepts in practice, have to their credit a product in girls and boys of which they may be proud, for undoubtedly they have given India professional leaders in many directions. They have sought to develop character with ability, to embellish insight with experience, to teach style and add beauty to the business of living.

All this is admirable. And the roundedness of the education that you have given our boys and girls has added to the richness of our relatively barren lives in India. I have met several of the children whom your institutions have turned out in the course of my 18 years of educational administration in the Union Ministry of Education, and more recently, I have met, taught and known them in two colleges of Delhi: St. Stephen's and the Jesus and Mary College. And I can testify to the quality of your instruction and education.

In view of all this, I consider it unwise to underestimate the Public Schools as some public figures have done or to destroy what we cannot afford to re-create. It is, however, equally unwise to overlook or to turn a deaf ear or blind eye to the criticism that is levelled against, the Public Schools, for that way desiccation and death lie. For my part, I want you to live and to continue to shape the lives of our children, but of all our children and not just a chosen few.

And so you must allow me to start by enunciating a fundamental proposition in education that will enable us to see whether there is anything after all in the public criticisms now so current about the Public Schools of India. And if so, what measure of truth they contain that we need to act upon.

First, no education at any level is good, bad or indifferent in itself and without reference to a specific environment. A form of education that may suit the State of New York is not necessarily suitable for the more backward parts of Indiana, though both New York and Indiana are States within the United States of America, the same far-flung country, with approximately the same history and the same Constitution, the same general outlook, the same language, the same idiom of living. Schools are good or bad or indifferent only in relation to the society they serve and the times within which they educate. The Public Schools of India will be judged good, bad or indifferent, not by their record of service in the past, not because of their special facilities in the present, but by their relevance to society in India and to the year 1978.

What is Indian society like in 1978? Indian society is governed by two major stereotypes, the preliminary with which we start all teaching in Indian Area Studies. The two stereotypes are the Map and the Hour Glass. The map stands for the area of the country that is more than a country. For India is a subcontinent, about equal in area to the whole of Europe less the USSR. When you recall the diversity of Europe and its divisions you should have no difficulty accounting for the diversity and the divisions of India. The hour glass stands for history and accounts for the fact that our 610 millions today live in different centuries at one and the same time. Combine these two stereotypes and you have a society that is multi-regional, multi-religious, multi-linguistic, multicultural and deeply stratified socially and economically. But—and this is of the utmost importance—in 1950 we, the Indian People, gave to ourselves a Constitution in which we called ourselves a Sovereign Democratic Republic. In due course we described ourselves as a democratic, socialistic, and secular Republic. And there is no going back on this. There is, indeed, a compulsion to go forward in reflecting these elements. The compulsion is on everyone in this country, but I think it probably weighs more heavily on educationists than on anyone else. For it is we who make the mind and personality of this country's children, and it is these children who will inherit the land.

Somewhat earlier I referred to the differences that obtained in the States of New York and Indiana though they are both integral parts of the USA. We, like the Americans, are a far-flung people, a continental people, who have to educate Tripura as well as Delhi, Assam and NEFA as well as Bombay, the heart of Madhya Pradesh as well as the coastal areas of Tamil Nadu. So it may well be argued that a uniform standardised system and a typical school are beside the point. Here, I would agree with you. I would say that the size and diversity of India make it possible for us to have all kinds of school education at the same time, in different places, but the range will always be limited by what the whole society proposes as its distinctive features. Our society has reached the point at which it is insistently democratic, socialistic and secular.

A society such as ours has both centrifugal and centripetal tendencies. The former tend towards disintegration and have to be checked. The latter tend towards cohesion and have to be promoted. It follows, if we accept my initial axiom that schools are good only in relation to the society that they serve and times within which they educate, that schools which, by their essential character isolate their children from the mainstream of Indian life, are moving in the wrong direction for our society. Those that consciously bridge the gap between those who wield power and govern, and those who do not wield power, are relevant and good.

There is probably more discussion and more fruitful discussion about the meaning of democracy today in India then there has ever been. We are today a truly interesting country to live in, and a truly instructive country to listen to. For we understand, as we seem not to have fully understood these last 30 years, that political democracy, vital as it is, is just not enough. There is a certain minimum standard of living below which no human being should be required or permitted to live in 1978. We have not achieved this minimum standard. Though within the Constitution, several millions aged 21 and above cast their votes to choose their leaders once in five years, they are still without the minimum that, defines life in modern terms. They subsist. That they truly live, we cannot claim. And this is a fact that has to be placed daily, hourly before our privileged children in Public Schools.

More: any government that wants to survive in this country can do so only by meeting this excruciating economic challenge. It is not enough to have the political rights that we have today, though these are vitally important. Let no one delude any of us that these rights do not underlie further democratic development. When we were denied these rights during the Emergency for 20 months, we began truly to understand what freedom meant. Speaking for myself, I was acutely miserable, and I mean just that. Acutely miserable. So we have to work to keep this flame alive. But even with the rule of law, with freedom of conscience and expression, with the independence of the judiciary secured, total freedom from censorship in press and mass media, we have still not realised the other imperative of democracy: that economic imperative, that develops logically into socialism. Liberal socialism, for there is no need, as I see it, for massive state control. The liberal socialism that obtains in Britain today, with the necessary adaptations to India, will give us the link that many of us seek between political and economic democracy.

How does all this affect the Public Schools of India? Why are they especially under attack today? When we think of economic democracy and the masses of children still out of school, the 70 per cent of illiteracy with which this society is burdened, the demands of a modern society and the need to produce wealth, we think of the unused potential that lies in illiterate children. A society that publicly enunciates its goals in the immediate future is automatically under an obligation to demonstrate its means of increasing productivity through education and ensuring equality of opportunity, an equal claim for everyone to the means of learning and living, working and achieving, the good life,:

Today, the children who are able to get to Public Schools are automatically plainly ahead in this race to obtain the means of livelihood. They come of better homes, are better instructed, better set up physically, have enjoyed better facilities in study—libraries, games, total environment, not merely than the thousands at less well equipped schools,—state schools all over the country—but also the millions of children as yet outside any school system, for whom we have not provided at all. Those who insist in equality of opportunity as the cornerstone of our Constitution cannot well overlook the citadels of privilege that the Public Schools still represent. We have not merely to be egalitarian, we have to demonstrate that we are. Apart from a small number of scholars financed by a government grant, children at Public Schools belong to a socio-economic elite that lives apart from the masses of India. And so the temptation exists for politicians to talk of abolishing Public Schools. You may have heard this reiterated recently to prove that the government is fundamentally egalitarian. The Public Schools, as they are, must attract this kind of utterance.

Does this mean that your entire frame of reference, your inspiration dating back to Arnold or earlier, your passion for the twin development of ability and character-and-personality, your concepts of leadership must be destroyed? No, I do not think so. At least not entirely, for revolution has seemed to me to lie less in destruction than in the swift transformation of an attitude of mind. When Public Schools respond to the cry of "Indianise" by introducing snippets of Indian culture— Hindi, and Indian music and Indian dancing— they are missing the essential point. The cry to "Indianise" is an appeal less to culture than to conscience It is to demonstrate a feeling of oneness with all the people of the country.

I recall an American educationist who had lived and worked for years in India at Delhi, when I met him in 1971 in the US and shared a platform with him on education, saying: "Splendid things have happened in free India. Undoubtedly what democratisation has taken place, has taken place since independence. But the thing I miss so profoundly in education is the general feeling of: 'These—all these—are our children'" And of course he was right.

If we felt as strongly about all our children as parents feel about their children, and school managements feel about their children, this would be a very different country. It is because we seem unable to extend our allegiance from family or school or clan to the masses we see but do not know, that we are guilty of the paradox of professing economic democracy but practising the worst kind of oligarchy.

If, then, the Public Schools are not to stand abolished and not to stand out as landmarks of elitism due for demolition, what are they to do? There are at least two big aims that dominate school education anywhere. They are to develop the individual qua individual; and to produce good citizens. These objectives are not imcompatible. In the first place, we do what the Public Schools have tried to do: we develop the many-sided child via Socrates. We teach him/her to think clearly, to think steadily, to think truly, to think deeply and we apply our thinking constantly to living. Next, we have to develop social responsibility to the point that our privileged children see their advantages and deplore the absence of these same advantages among the millions who stand without in the cold or the heat. A social conscience is necessary baggage for our times. To have and not to be aware that millions have not, is to be handicapped, to be retarded and, worst of all, to be out of step with the times. The Public Schools must understand the temper of the times. Their instruction may be modern; their attitudes are not.

How do we make educated individuals who are also educated citizens? By recognising two sorts of responsibility: the responsibility to develop oneself to the hilt of one's powers, and the responsibility to harness these powers to the public service. Here are some of the ways in which Public Schools can attune themselves to our society and the times.

First, enter today upon a scientific evaluation of your schools. Set out and re-set out your objectives in education and do not let them be too abstract or too general. Instead, frame your objectives to fit the needs of our society and our times. We can no longer set ourselves to turn out gentlemen for gentlemanly pursuits, for the era of leisure is over. We need working men and women who, by their expertise, their initiative and adaptability, their social courage and involvement, their vocational skills will be able to transform India from a medieval into a modern society. It is not enough to take comfort from being the tenth most industrialised society in the world, for this means little relative to the employment of our millions, the education for work of our 90 million or so children. We need schemes and projects for educating people in rural and urban areas for work, to ensure that they can live, instead of subsist, for the rest of their lives. The bias in favour of practicality and vocational education is irresistible and must form part of your blueprint for improvement in 1978.

This process of evaluation, of stating and restating school objectives must be done at least once a year. The whole management and faculty and selected children should be involved in it, so that the school becomes a community of learning-and-doing capable of influencing its neighbourhood while the children are still with you. You must develop among them social responsibility, and social responsibility is not developed in the hothouse of the school classroom. The school must go out into the closest rural neighbourhood and take learning to the most convenient rural area. This is not a matter of charity, but of obligation. It is also a way to silence your critics. Adopt a village and enable it to understand and enjoy the fruits of healthy living. Adopt a poor school and, by feeding it with your facilities, make it a good school. This has been done effectively in Tamil Nadu. Why not in the north of India?

Next, the Public Schools have claimed that they educate for leadership. But concepts of leadership have undergone a fundamental change. The Public School type of leadership is no longer highly valued. We have to eliminate altogether the concept of "Class 5" as determining the capacity to lead. The time has come to develop a meritocracy. I mentioned earlier that schools that assist the process of integration are good, those that isolate themselves from the mainstream, bad. The Public Schools have integrated boys and girls of the same socio-economic class. This is horizontal integration. But they have done little to integrate vertically. I have spent 18 years in governmental administration and I know now, as I did not know earlier, that the upper classes of India cannot effectively administer people whom they do not know. In our stratified society, the classes do not get to know one another till forcibly confronted. Till at least one-fourth of your enrolment is from the weaker sections of society, i.e. are merit-cum-means scholars, these classes go unrepresented in the school community. And the upper class continues to live its isolated life away from a knowledge of the under-privileged. The gulf has to be bridged, and the earlier the better. Let the number of scholarships be progressively increased. Finance them out of an Endowment Fund that ought to be established early with the assistance of rich parents. The Fund has the merit of conferring independence of government grants. Out of this reconstructed school society, a new leadership, better related to our times must emerge, Films like Shyam Benegal's *Manthan* have the right idea and should be screened over and over again and then discussed in the classroom. Till something like his intimate concern for the well-being of a village emerges, the class gap will remain, and the wrong kind of old-time leadership persist. The new leadership is without patronage. It is a primus-inter-pares relationship.

Thirdly, the Public Schools are instructionally good schools and since you are better placed than most schools to develop early the seeds of professionalism among boys and girls, do just this. What does it imply? Three things: (i) competence involving knowledge and skills at international level (ii) the continuing cultivation of excellence with the 'divine discontent' that means one is never self-satisfied or complacent, (iii) the habit of translating theoretic knowledge into practice in living situations.

One of the most distressing defects of our society is the ease with which people are satisfied with their performance. Boys and girls of 17 in India are much less well-informed than their counterparts in Britain and America, much less independent, much less determined to live their lives without the support and protection of parents and relatives. We must recover from makeshift ways, and the Public Schools can well lead such a movement in favour of early professionalism.

Fourthly, within the group of Public Schools, there is now a need to cultivate special identity for individual schools and specialisations in, for example, science, the social studies, languages and vocational skills, that will promote excellence. In this pursuit of excellence, much more has to be done with libraries to cultivate the reading habit, to make our children better informed about India and the world. I worry more about the inadequacies among girls than boys, because parents still regard their sons as potential householders and train them for full-time employment. But girls must be trained for work in India as seriously as boys and must recover from the superstition that marriage is a profession. It is no longer so and, in my view, should never have been.

I cannot over-emphasise the need for urgent self-scrutiny and reform. The changes that I suggest are urgent because the Public Schools have grown to be regarded as impediments to democratic reconstruction. Today, it is a case of "reform or revolutionise." No one will regret more than I, the attempt to take you over or to abolish you, but both alternatives are now on the cards. Now that you have come together in conference, look the situation clearly in the face and steal your critics' thunder by democratising yourselves, while ensuring that you remain good schools for the times. If you can take under-privileged children and make scholars and good citizens of them, you have demonstrated that you care about survival, better than volumes in praise of your services. Some part of your inheritance, the dated part, will have to be abandoned. Study this inheritance to see what you can afford to shed, what you must keep to be true to yourselves as good schools. But come to terms with your society and the times. For your survival is at stake.

So far I have argued from reason for the need for swift adaptation. I now make a different appeal. I am as embarrassed as anyone by reiterated pronouncements of patriotism. Genuine patriots rarely talk about love of country, they manifest it in action. But a developing society such as ours cannot achieve its goals without some sacrifice, individual and collective. This is not an appeal to rational social justice but to something larger, the will to sacrifice for what one values. All of us are touched in diverse ways by the image of India. We have to prove this feeling. Here is a parable for our times that must speak for me.

A young man who appeared some years ago for his viva in the IAS/IFS examination was splendid by any measure. He was a Public School boy of some distinction, a leader at Elphinstone College and later at St. Stephen's; a Rhodes Scholar who took a Law degree when up at Christ Church, Oxford,

He appeared for his written papers (IAS/IFS) and acquitted himself with distinction. At his interview he seemed almost too good to be true, and his Board very wisely decided to test his authenticity with an unexpected question. "Mr. X, what is your concept of Patriotism?" He was a thoughtful young man, and he thought his way through this one. He said: "Today, it is clearly not the flamboyant or heroic thing it once was. It is quieter, an awareness of what is necessary, a commitment. Perhaps, I would define it as "Service without vanity".

If the Public Schools of India can accept service without vanity as their motto for the future and act in accordance with it, they will have cut the ground from under their critics' feet. What is more, they will be acknowledged as the pacesetters of school education for this troubled country of ours.

24

Co-Educational Colleges vs Women's Colleges*

A developing society such as India has distinctive features that demand special attention in educational planning. But it is just as serious a mistake to concentrate on these distinctive features to the exclusion of world experience and attitudes, as it is to adopt in India, without suitable adaptation, practices that have paid off in the developed world. To persist in maintaining and promoting women's colleges in India today is to make the first mistake, i.e. to accord to specifically Indian vulnerability an indulgence that we ought to have withdrawn decades ago.

For it is clearly a vulnerability in 1977-78 that women of particular sections of Indian society feel safer in women's colleges than they do in their co-educational counterparts. Indeed, the conception of safety is misplaced in our times and in our generally law-abiding society. Why should girls of between 18 and 23 years of age in large cities and towns feel safer in a women's college than in a co-educational college? Because these girls and women are still not attuned to the society of men. By continuing to provide girls with this protection, we continue to perpetuate false fears and that unnatural division

* *New Frontiers in Education*, January—March 1978.

of society that all modern psychology teaches us to deplore. The net result of this protective segregation is to perpetuate fear of the male sex among women, and to attribute to men predatory instincts that, by and large, civilisation has cured or at least held in check for some centuries.

One of the historical arguments often cited for special institutions for women at college level is the story of women's polytechnics in India. When the polytechnic was open to both men and women, there was, so it is reported, a trickle only of women students. Then, special women's polytechnics were set up, and an avalanche of women swept in to join them. The answer to this historical argument is that things have changed substantially for the better in the last 20 years. The middle class woman needs to earn, and the polytechnics offer early material returns. In general, women will come to co-educational polytechnics if we do not provide them with too-easy alternatives.

Not merely is the fear that men will be violent to young women groundless; it is also restrictive, because it insulates women from that constant and natural intercourse with men in social and intellectual pursuits that benefits both sexes. A woman who can compete with men and hold her own with them is someone who has often been stretched beyond the competition offered her by her own sex in women's colleges. I am not suggesting for a moment that men are intrinsically more profound or powerful of intellect than women. This is a notion that was exploded decades ago. But it is surely clear that because men have enjoyed greater liberty in the exercise of their minds and bodies for centuries, they have been exposed to stimuli and to corrective experiences that have developed their minds to a level and a degree of assurance, strength and mastery that few women have achieved, for precisely the lack of these outlets and aids. To protect either sex beyond the natural age of protection is to abridge development. Boys have ordinarily been exposed to the hazards of survival, physical and mental, when they have attained maturity and even earlier. Girls and women in India frequently enjoy less freedom after they mature than before. And this is against all reason. The experience of womanhood is as important as the experience of manhood: both are maturing. To put the clock back for women once they have matured physically is to deny them the full intellectual and psychological fruits of this experience.

The case for co-education vs separate education for girls and boys at any level has, I believe, been proved in many countries of the world. The mainstream of school education in Britain and the US—I refer to the system of public education that is state-supported, and not to private schools with private endowments that can indulge an outmoded eccentricity—is co-educational. I have taught in the main school system of two states in America, New York and Indiana, and can testify to the fact that the intellectual and social cross-fertilisation that is evident there is good for everyone. Girls and boys take each other for granted. They are aware of sex as they approach maturity, and their interest in sex reflects the interest that their society takes in this physiological fact. But co-education destroys once and for all the furtive curiosity in sex that obtains in India, and that may well grow to be diseased, and it develops instead a healthy outgoing attitude to the other sex. At college level, there is no room for curiosity; the facts of sex have been mastered in adolescence. The minds of girls, as these are exposed to us in such places as the Harvard Law School, make it clear that, given the opportunity to work, think and study with men, girls can hold their own and can develop those traits that we in India still mistakenly describe, with ill-concealed appreciation, as 'masculine'.

So supposedly die-hard a university as Oxford has now made 16 of its men's colleges co-educational. Nothing will stem the tide of women's education in Britain; the bastions of male prejudice and monopoly have fallen before a regiment of highly scholarly women. The argument, is two fold: fundamental rights and economy. Nearer home, St. Stephen's College,

Delhi has opened its first degree courses to women without multiplying its disciplinary problems, and with every evidence of a more spirited, healthy and colourful campus. That the change was adopted primarily for economic reasons does not weaken the case for co-education. Indeed, in a country like India, economy is often a conclusive argument.

It is because the liberal and liberating attitude is effective and productive in education, that I so strongly support it. In this, as in so many other walks of life, segregation that implies external control, is stultifying and uneconomic. Once impose control, and the need to maintain that control is imperative and expensive. Walls divide as well as protect, "Something there is", wrote Robert Frost, "that does not love a wall". The opposite view that self-contained colleges for the sexes are good, is based on the wooden and unproven assumption that "good fences make good neighbours". The first adage stands for the forward-looking view in education and life; the second, for unthinking conservatism that such countries as India cannot afford.

In India the continued insistence on women's colleges is based on a many-sided fear. Fear, that girl students will in some way be corrupted by contact with boys; fear, that women on the staff will have to compete with men and will not be able to hold their own with men: fear among managements that problems of discipline will multiply, and that the women-managers themselves will not be equal to man-management. This self-creating spiral of fear, even where women are not plainly conscious of it, reinforces the desire to continue to have women's colleges and makes it a vested interest. The last argument that I have sometimes heard used even in the US and by such Women's Lib leaders as Gloria Steinem, supports women's colleges because they offer women the security of a territory of their own, help the inarticulate among them to develop confidence and act as a sort of apprenticeship for public life in which women may graduate from the simple competition with other women, to the more complex competition of a man's world.

It seems to me that if we are to break this species of fear, we ought to do so right away and not in stages. Nothing except a drastic break with a single-sex college, men's or women's, will bring the two sexes into open communication and competition with each other. But if we must make concessions to the 'hasten slowly' people, the way to do so, is to insist that teachers in an either exclusively men's or exclusively women's college shall be of both sexes; that both men and women will be free to compete for these teaching places and the best woman/man win. If again, there is the fear in the initial stages of the changeover that men will dominate the staffroom of an erstwhile women's college, some provision could be made temporarily only for a 50:50 ratio of women to men on the staff.

To what extent are the minds of Indian women and men so different at college level that we need to bear these differences in mind in college planning? In India, the differences are more marked than in developed societies because Indian society has deliberately accentuated the differences, has done practically nothing to slur over them and nothing to induce either sex to go in for disciplines that are supposedly natural to the one or the other sex. How many men in India have been induced to read Home Science? And how many women, Aeronautical Engineering? All enlightened Commissions, not excluding the 1966 Education Commission headed by Dr. Kothari, have advocated the same curricula for women and men at college level. By perpetuating the theory of separate excellences, propensities and skills, we do some injury to both sexes. The only scientific way to plan is to base planning on the enunciated objective, to develop the full intellectual potentiality of both sexes. The fully developed woman will, once developed, cease automatically to be a mere sex-object. The emphases in both her private and her public life will change for the better. All our limiting superstitions about what women are capable of doing will crumble sway. Not long ago, a woman was supposed to be incapable of understanding higher mathematics. Madame, Curie was constantly cited as the exception that proved the rule that women were unfit for physics. Contrariwise, the notion that women are more literary than men has been constantly falsified in fact, but persists in the notion that women are especially suited to a discipline that implies sensibility, a gentle perception and the subtle use of words. After all, was there not Jane Austen, etc.?

Such a superstition is an affront both to the concept of literature as a 'gentle' discipline that does not require the constant use of the corroding reason, as it is to women as being better suited to this than to the tougher rationality demanded by science. If we allow our educational planning to be based on the popular fallacies that our society has in its weakness perpetuated, we will do nothing to enlarge the world of a woman's mind, her initiative, her character, personality and life. For all these, she has now to go audaciously down into the arena of life as it is in the modern world, without diffidence, without self-consciousness, without apology. Unless we prepare her to do this in college by declining to set up more women's colleges, and insist instead that our girls go to co-educational institutions, we make ourselves a party to retarding the full development of Indian women. Incidentally, we also retard their contribution to the nation's development.

25

Teaching and Learning the Humanities in Indian Colleges*

The Humanities are among the oldest subjects taught in Indian colleges. Methods of reaching them, though not normally a discipline at college level, have been written on ad nauseam. Most of us know what makes a good college in teaching and learning. And yet the entire subject is rendered complex by three factors:

(i) The state of the humanities in India today.

(ii) The state of college teaching in India today.

(iii) The special conditions and obligations of a good college, such as those represented here, in India today.

In short, it is the special circumstances of our country and times that make the subject thought-provoking.

It is customary in discussing the humanities and the social sciences to say that they have suffered academically in proportion as science and technology have prospered by the climate of modernisation and industrialisation that theoretically prevails in India. The arguments are now familiar. The best students read science or technology. Those who cannot, read the social studies, accent on economics for business

---

* A paper read at the Isabella Thoburn College, Lucknow, in 1976.

management, and history for the Indian Administrative Service. At several good colleges, history and economics are treated as stepping stones to the all-India services. The humanities, variously defined to mean language and literature with a special bias, outside Uttar Pradesh, in favour of English language and literature, are considered by those proposing to practise journalism (a misconception that it would be as well to dispel early, since historians, political scientists, economists and scientists frequently make better journalists than students of literature...) copy-writing, teaching, publishing and writing. All these, except teaching, are relatively new professions. The market for them is limited. The rewards are moderate unless you have unusual luck. They are, for the most part, man-dominated professions in which women, many of whom wish to read the humanities because they are genuinely interested in them, are not always or even generally valued at par with men. And so the strictly utilitarian value of the humanities is at a discount. From the remarks of students, girls and boys, of literature ranging from "His father has plenty of money; he is here for culture" to "Oh! She'll marry the moment she takes her degree", you'd have thought that those studying the humanities were not likely to be serious scholars! One of them remarks loftily to those asking how he combines a part-time job with the study of English Literature: " I can do this because I'm just reading English. I've plenty of time".

But almost worse, because so much more harmful, is the attitude of those who teach the humanities in Indian colleges today. In the first place, I ought to say that I am confining myself to colleges. I am not straying into University teaching, which also leaves something to be desired, but in which there are still people sufficiently well qualified and sufficiently professional of attitude towards research, teaching and that constant refreshing that is implied in both, that it is not in such a bad state. College teaching-and-learning is fundamentally undergraduate teaching with tutoring at MA, level. Few colleges make provision for lecturing at Master's level though of course a college may be a venue for such a course of lectures.

What is right and what wrong today with college teaching of the humanities in India? I would say that the right things are that in the better colleges of India, there is still order in the physical sense and method in dealing with a curriculum, that is still largely university-imposed, and in which teachers, partly through their own lack of initiative, have had little say. Student-material, relative to what is available in that geographic area, is good. Both girls and boys who can get into a good college with a tradition, do so partly for instruction, partly for tradition and a climate of discipline. Where some admission test is taken, large numbers of students, most of them good, are turned away, so it would be possible to argue that the student-material is good and, to this extent, that teaching has a reasonable chance of achieving results. Yet is the teaching what it should be in 1976? That really is the question. And my answer is "No," a categorical "No."

What is wrong with it? It may enter the profession with scholarship and the ability to communicate it, and this may last for a year or two. With early tenure comes an almost inevitable relaxation. The same things are said in the same way, year after year with marginal differences. Many college teachers are still not above dictating notes that they inherited from a revered teacher, who possibly also took notes and dictated them. Librarians tell me that Faculty scarcely uses the library. Perhaps, you will say, it is given to buying its own books, and I have been agreeably surprised to find that there are some colleges in which this is in fact so. Staff is anxious to renew its knowledge in criticism and so does read (buying its own books) but it does not necessarily keep up with modern writing in various genres. It reads round the curriculum which is frequently, by world standards, hopelessly out-of-date and an impediment, to the perfection of a modern language. Invited to serve an Advanced Course that brings the university curriculum up-to-date in progressive colleges, at least five out of every ten members of a humanities/faculty will dodge speaking on writing published between 1930 and 1976. The curriculum ends often at 1930 though it describes this part of its activity as "20th Century Literature". This is distressing. I have sat on selection committees in which lecturers in English Literature have not been aware of the modern writers to whom candidates refer in the course of the discussion conducted at an admission interview. It is essential that faculty in the humanities keeps up with modern writing that ranks as literature. The comparative habit of mind is implied in all literary criticism and must be projected into writing reviewed in 1976, where the books are obtainable in India. The use of a library that can afford to keep up with book-purchase on a large scale is, therefore, absolutely essential. This is possibly conceded in good colleges as a form, but it is not practised with that automatic use that one would have a right to expect. The result is that students are frequently dismayed at finding that they know more about modern writing than their lecturers do.

There is a superstition in Indian colleges that language and literature are two distinct disciplines, and that expertise in literature implies only a knowledge of literary writing, but does not necessarily extend to a mastery of the language for either speaking or writing purposes. I constantly run into Indian graduates of literature who can be depended on to 'place' abstruse passages in prose or poetry in English and other European literatures, and have plainly treated literature as an intellectual discipline. Nevertheless, these same graduates do not write the language whose literature they have studied so diligently, either with complete correctness or with that degree of sophistication that we are entitled to expect of those who have studied literature at college level for three or four years. When it is pointed out that the language in which they discuss literary problems is imperfect, inept, dated and, in the adverse sense, 'literary' and 'academic', they smile or shrug their shoulders as if disclaiming responsibility: Language, that's a detail, they seem to say. But is it? There can be no expertise in literature that does not subsume a total ease and at-homeness in the corresponding language. There can be no literature that does not imply the ability to innovate in the language to which it belongs. There can be no literature for those who do not sense and master the genius of a language, so that they do not require footnotes on the subtle use of words or phrases. Myths, imagery, symbolism that play an important part in all literature, must be assumed to be self-explanatory once a first degree in literature has been taken. Not to be able to read between the lines, or to listen between the lines, is not to have found the key to literature. There are graduates in English literature and Masters, too, from Indian universities and colleges, who are employed in the all-India services, in journalism, in publishing and in teaching, in many of whom it is patent that a knowledge of literature has been acquired without any corresponding at-homeness in language. Neither the written nor the spoken word has been mastered. Yet metaphysical discussion at some length and of some complexity is conducted with a flourish and an ostentation that eloquently overlooks the need for accuracy and mastery of the basic elements of language. Some years ago, I mean about 20 years ago, one quick measure of whether or not you were educated, was the facility with which you could use the language in which you chose to express yourself. The general decline of excellence in the use of language is a noticeable feature of contemporary education in India, and it is a shortcoming that few educational institutions are doing anything to correct as a routine practice.

The falling off that is so manifest in communication is often considered unimportant, when compared with the defective content of college education in India I do not think it is unimportant; it is symptomatic of the greatly enhanced slovenliness that presides over our educational lives. Till this is corrected with the automatic precision with which a child is taught how to brush his teeth the right way, we are no nearer securing the substructure of an efficient basis for learning in the humanities.

The Christian colleges of India serve a student population overwhelmingly non-Christian, and many members of their faculties are also non-Christians. It is a tribute to these colleges that non-Christian students throng their portals and are willing to use almost any connection to obtain admission to them. This argues something that will bear scrutiny. Not all Christian colleges are of the same level of excellence, but it is clearly an asset to be a member of this group, for to be comparable with it implies in the public mind (i) a tradition of relative efficiency in teaching and learning (ii) a tradition in discipline (iii) an inculcation of standards of behaviour that do not ordinarily obtain elsewhere. The teacher-student relationship does both credit and continues when the student has left the college. Loyalty to such colleges is generally strong. Old Students' Associations are willingly built up and the inflow of a student population with father and grandfather affiliations is not infrequent.

In the Indian situation all this is good, but it is hedged round with dangers at the present time. For one thing, the goodness is relative only (I will return to this later). Where all around is in a state of decrepitude, slovenliness and makeshift, fit is not so difficult to be noticed because one's standards are higher. It is never sufficiently emphasised in India that in creating and maintaining standards, we compete not with the average in India, but with the best in the world. The standard of comparison must be for 1976, and it must be international. Maintenance is expensive and more: it argues an attention to detail that goes against some basic element in our national make-up. What is new today is soiled tomorrow. Our homes reflect this deep-seated carelessness, the habit of slipshodness that every foreigner expects to see on landing at Palam. Our schools and colleges that have a public, as well as a private obligation to invite admiration and interest are dark, dusty and singularly unattractive. This may seem a triviality when compared mentally with mass poverty, starvation and indiscipline, but is in fact an important introduction to the life of a college. The Jesus and Mary College, New Delhi is a comparatively new institution in Chanakyapuri. It has a charming campus that is magnificently maintained, yet it has no more money than anyone else. The management has had its usual share of troubles with teams of sweepers who hold it periodically up to ransom. When the sweepers do not turn up, the nuns have themselves swept and swabbed floors till you can see yourself mirrored in them. They have an educational stake in cleanliness: from the daily demonstration of it, students learn how homes and institutions ought to be maintained. St. Stephen's College. Delhi, is now a hundred years old, and has an old red-brick building that recalls Keble College, Oxford, or Girton, Cambridge. It is not the shining new landscape of architecture that confronts you at JMC, but it is a delight to teach and learn in. Its day-to-day maintenance leaves nothing, but nothing, to be desired.

I do not ask for glass-and-chromium, for the demonstrated affluence of the affluent world that we have not got. I ask for what we can afford in India. It is folly to play down externals when you are seeking to cultivate taste and add to the richness of human life For this is the function of the humanities, The newcomer to the college, parent or student, forms that first impression that pays dividends, on externals. Detail in maintenance is a pointer to the seriousness with which a college means to live its daily life. There is a community of interest to live in cleanliness and beauty, that is contagious, and that is an integral part of a humanistic education.

What has all this to do with the teaching of the humanities? A great deal. We have had visiting us at St. Stephen's recently, a Professor of English Poetry from Yale, who argues that it is possible to see poetry as a "survival technique." He is talking of the need to develop in education a living counterpoise to the analytic disciplines of logic, mathematics and science, to develop a technology of what he calls respect, to offset the technology of manipulation. The latter makes practical men, engineers and craftsmen; the former makes artists, creative and intuitive spirits who supply the private world of human identity, self-knowledge, penetration to the depths of human consciousness that together justify the teaching and learning of the humanities. Whether we use the humanities in the broad sense to be convertible with the Arts of Indian universities, or in the more restricted sense of language, literature and the fine arts only, we have often to deal with the intangibles that do not yield immediate marketable results, nor, indeed, the sort of certainty that the physical sciences require. In consequence, they tend in all science-dominated modern societies to be underestimated and under-paid. A poet is generally a poor man; an engineer a prosperous one. A teacher of the arts is a comparatively poor citizen, and the avenues of employment are limited in developing societies for arts students.

As the economic rewards of science and technology are larger than the humanities, so the investment in them is larger. It seems to me that the last refuge of the humanities and humanitarianism (for they are, or should be, connected) is, or should be, a Christian or similar college. Through the 36 years of my professional life, through all the transitions in educational and economic enchantment and disenchantment, planning and unplanning, that it has been my doubtful privilege to experience, I have never had the smallest reason to lose faith in the teaching and learning of the humanities. Perhaps this is because I have had the opportunity to be taught by, and to learn from people of many nationalities, who have lived in accordance with their beliefs. A dedication to the humanities is a dedication to a way of life, and it is frequently not a paying way of life. It pays in purely material terms to turn away from history and literature, from philosophy and even psychology (other than clinical psychology), to the utilitarian studies—economics, commerce, business management. The skills are more immediately encashable than the arts. I am not less practical than the next woman, and women are extremely practical. A developing society needs executives, technicians and technologists. But no man or woman is educated who is ignorant of the humanities, and no man or woman is fit to lead, to rule, to administer or to teach who has not at some time been grounded in the humanities or the values that they seek to inculcate for life. Science may dictate the logical thing to do; the humanities dictate the honourable thing to do, the sensitive thing to feel. No man or woman is whole who has neglected the humanities, and it is at the peril of society that their study is neglected to make possible the monopolistic triumphs of science.

Perhaps it requires both an old civilisation such as ours, and colleges such as ours to see the need to combine the two cultures of science and the humanities without detriment to either, and with an instinct to keep pace with the times. If the last decade has taught us anything in college education, it is that academic pigeonholes are bad things, that knowledge, that was once fragmented, must now come together, be cross-fertilised with a multi-disciplinary approach. There is no effective study of literature, for instance, without history; no profitable study of history without its corresponding literature. There is no mastery of a traditional novel without an inter-disciplinary approach supplied by not literature only, but also history, sociology, psychology, philosophy and politics. Christian colleges are in a better position to advocate and achieve this broad spectrum of learning and teaching, because faculty forms a community that can adapt itself swiftly to new college programmes. The habit of teamwork is healthy and can be expanded and promoted without the hysteria of revolution. Team-teaching and other experiments of this sort are more feasible in Christian colleges than elsewhere because faculty is more dedicated, more adaptable, more involved in educational innovation.

Innovation—there, you knew I was coming to it. Now that the word is out of the bag, I ought to pursue it with appropriate fanaticism. For the last four years, I have been teaching at a good Christian college, and for the last two years, I have been teaching at two good Christian colleges, one very old, the other very new. I am of the view that we are teaching on the lines on which our admirable grandfathers taught—methodically, substantially but unimaginatively for the times. The times demand much more. For knowledge has multiplied, there has been a revolution in science and technology, the mass media of communication and, indeed, education. The paperback has come to stay. Among those acclimatised to reading, skills are now very sharp. There are a few slow readers among Honours students at good Christian colleges. This being so, the old methods are not good enough. A lecturer must be astoundingly good and, in a scholarly sense, creative to be listened to with the rapt attention that lecturers demand of their audiences, A paper is sometimes listened to because it is assumed to be a work of discovery or original experience. But as emphasis has shifted from teaching to learning, learners have to be consistently associated with the business of discovery. I do not ask merely for student participation as we used to do in school. I ask for student initiative all the way, and to encourage this, teachers have to be courageous. Increasingly, attendance at lectures is poor. Increasingly, attendance at seminars is good. This has to be explained and cannot be dodged or explained away. To be listened to, teaching has to be creative, interesting and—yes, why not?—entertaining. There is some drudgery in all scholarship and in all preparation for examinations, but learning in general is not, and should not be, dull. But dull lecturers continue to exist, and as universities demand a certain percentage compulsory attendance from students, they, the teachers .that is, have a captive audience but an inattentive captive audience. Once the necessary percentage of attendance is obtained, students stay away, a manifest declaration of failure in teaching. And this is happening in Christian, as in other colleges.

The issue is not merely one of qualifications. It is one of missing empathy. In the first place, as I said earlier, teachers have to keep up with modern writing in their fields and sub-fields. They have to be contemporary in attitude, idea, concept and behaviour. They will then understand why they make or do not make an impact on their students. The days are gone when a student will accept a personal relationship between him and his teacher as a substitute for intellectual stimulus. Either the teacher will do his job as it requires to be done in 1976, or he will speak to an empty classroom. Such things have been known to happen in our so-called good colleges, and there are few experiences as humiliating to the professional teacher as a deserted classroom. Yet there are teachers who have so far lost respect for themselves that they can say: "Very well, it doesn't matter. I continue to draw my salary whether or not you attend my classes."

Student evaluation is essentially a good thing though it may be wrongly used. A management should never undertake this; teachers should. But it is not unknown for rivalry among faculty to make evaluation misleading. There is still in India, and possibly elsewhere, the lack of that professional attitude to college teaching, which rejoices in the expertise of others. I have known great triviality among members of the same department and of the same college. And this is a pity, because it tells permanently against the refinement of teaching and learning. If everyone has enough to do, there will be no scope for triviality of the kind I have in mind. But there generally are a few rather lazy members of staff who, though initially good, have come to be lethargic about teaching and would prefer a generally easy-going attitude to work, to the enthusiastic innovative energy that should dominate the teaching of the humanities in India today. To these people, innovative techniques spell danger; they are set against them. I say that Christian colleges have nevertheless to continue to struggle against the desiccated old methods. Till students can take over their own learning, teaching has to go on, but the idea is to hasten the date at which the student becomes independent, not to perpetuate his tutelage.

Part of the difficulty in learning is that we are still over-stressing the need for old-time teaching. The alternative, or at least one of the alternatives is here, under our noses, and we don't see it. I am referring to a library, and of the learning process of which the library should be the hub. Despite my 63 years, most of them spent in India, I am not a cynic or pessimist. If I were, I would forfeit my claim to being an educationist, for if tomorrow cannot be better than yesterday or today through us, the college teachers of India, why do we go on at all? The optimist by definition is someone who believes that something can be done to improve man. That is why we study the humanities. That is why we emphasise them; for learning, we imply, must be man-centred. Because I believe this, I constantly ask myself from where I shall draw my strength. And I now know in India, that there is more strength to be had from the wise dead whose books line my library shelves, than there is from the bumbling living who do not sufficiently value books. We serve the living certainly, and life here and now is larger than books, but we are in danger in the humanities in India of not being sufficiently knowledgeable to be able to mould minds. The humanities tend to be elusive, intangible. Between the lines, lies-knowledge more profound than in the lines. Symbols, images are every scrap as important as grammatical and syntactical meaning, indeed more so, in literature. It is easy to test the acquisition of knowledge in the precise sciences in which I include mathematics. Not so easy in the humanities. For knowledge is acquired here as much through the emotions as through the intellect, through insight and intuition as through logic. How is this to be achieved? Chiefly, through the reading habit. Next, through the writing habit. The reading habit implies the constant, discerning use of the library. Move your classroom into the library. Change the conditions of day-to-day learning from the lecture-podium in the classroom with its captive, sleepy audience to a round table in a book-centred library. Only, choose your books wisely and choose your leaders with discernment. Increasingly, train students to take over their own learning. When they can do without you, your job is done.

The constant use of writing through the tutorial system is essential in the teaching of the humanities. I have little faith in objective tests except for revision of specific encapsulable content. In the cultivation of taste, in the evolution of literary judgment and artistic awareness, objective methods are, for the most part, irrelevant. The issue is not the manipulation of words; it is the discovery by students of the total effectiveness of language in communication. That we have not succeeded todate proclaims itself from the mis-spoken and mis-written languages that we hear and read all round us. Nowhere is the pursuit of excellence so articulately neglected as it is in the study of language. But if it can be rescued, I believe that the colleges best equipped to achieve the rescue are the colleges such as those represented here today, with their tradition of academic ambition, their awareness of the need to create and maintain standards, their insistence on relating practice to theory, behaviour to learning, their concept of professionalism and their essential thrust forward towards continuous improvement.

All this is good, but it conceals a danger to which I said that I would return before I concluded. The chief psychological failing of Christian colleges in particular is their all too-pronounced awareness of their relative strengths in the Indian situation today. When every day underscores some new relative strength, it is hard not to grow mildly complacent. Yet this way, decay lies. No matter, members of these colleges are apt to say or think, how unsatisfactory we are, we are better than so-and-so. This is really not good enough. It is in effect the brink of the precipice. And so, let this be my final exhortation to you. The standards that you and I have to seek are world standards, not just Indian standards. Till our students can stand up in the most progressive areas of the world and demonstrate their superiority to others in ability, integrity, that total roundedness of personality that a good college of 1976 should seek, our comparative condition in India is worth little. We have to break that imaginary sea wall, or that Himalayan wall that subsists in our minds, and that cordons the Indian peninsula off from the rest of the forward-reaching world. Let me improve on John Milton and Thomas Wolfe and say "Look, not homeward, but outward, Angel, if you would see how imperfect you are". You look homeward to serve; you look outward to evaluate yourself and replenish yourself with strength for service without vanity. And when you have tested yourself against the treasure-house of the "round world's imagined corners", in the humanities, you will truly be a teacher. For I have come to believe that the supreme virtue in a teacher is continued dissatisfaction with himself, with his knowledge, his ability to communicate it, to penetrate to the heart of what the wise dead thought and what the living grope to say. The only unforgiveable sin in teaching the humanities is to be dead sure that you have succeeded.

26

Education in the Round*

To bring children, juveniles and adults within the orbit of education in some form, orthodox or otherwise, formal and non-formal, implies an all-out attack on every medium of communication. If we are serious about this education in the round, we will act as if on an educational war-footing, and use part-time communicators of all sorts in teaching, radio, television, the cinema, correspondence course writers, programme instructors et al to achieve our ends. The questions that confront us are:

(i) How to select priorities, within priorities, for a recent Education Ministers' Conference resolved on things that cannot all be done together equally effectively.

(ii) How to coordinate media of communication within each locality and/or each age-group so as to ensure that the work is done systematically and that confusion is not escalated into chaos.

If we proceed on educational common sense it would seem that those plans claim top priority in which important goals are most likely to be achieved most swiftly. Our goal since 1950 has been to provide schooling for children in age-group 6-14. We have not been able to do so by 1977 for several reasons, some of them acceptable. But this is, for many reason, still the topmost priority.

---

* Earlier published in *The Education Quarterly, 1977-78.*

For one thing, it is normal and easy to begin to educate children in preference to adolescents or adults. A child's normal activity would take him/ her to school, whether in town or village. The school in a village is a physical landmark; the school in town is a symbol as well as a landmark. It is easy or relatively easy of access. Schooling at this stage is free. At six years of age neither a boy nor a girl is particularly valuable at home. Both can be dispensed with, and the mother feels freer for their absence. Above all, and this is the authentic educational argument, a child, other things being equal, is at the best stage for learning. A child retained in school till 14, is probably literate for life.

We have had approximately 30 years of experience seeking to bring children of between 6 and 14 years of age within the orbit of formal schooling. In the past, rightly or wrongly, we have conceived of this as the only way to educate. I cannot think that we were so misguided in principle, for the fact is that children assembled in manageable numbers in a school probably learn more quickly and permanently than if served in their homes or in ad hoc situations near their homes. The sheer discipline of going to school at a regular time, working to a timetable on a set pattern with other children of the same age, doing the same thing, listening to the same instruction, is probably good for everyone. It is one thing to say that we can no longer insist on this, because it has not proved capable of realisation, and quite another to say that it does not matter whether the child of six is taught this way or in another non-formal way.

Non-formal education is only short of a counsel of despair. The school has not succeeded in inducing ail children to come to it. In consequence, the school must go to the children.

What are the non-formal ways that we could use to remedy this situation?

Before we answer this, it is as well to clarify that non-formal, too, is structured education. There is a notion among the uninitiated that non-formal means 'where possible' and 'anyhow'. These are curious interpretations, because if the non-formal method is to work, it must be demonstrated to be a well-thought out and structured method that is more, not less, exacting than the normal school method. It demands greater intelligence and initiative on the part of the teacher, greater willingness to adapt him/herself to the child and the situation and to make the best of what is possible in time and attention. It is not ideal, but it is the best possible way out of a no-education-at-all alternative.

I have conducted no experiments on radio with small children and so cannot tell whether radio would really be effective with six-year olds. Television, on the other hand, to the extent that we can make it available, has been proved to be enormously effective in other countries. In India, it is not always available and it requires time and money to achieve expertise in teaching by TV. Even so, we should use what is available to develop programmes of subject-teaching and learning through television. More experiment is necessary with radio, but in the 11-14 age-group, radio could be made effective and, since it is available on a much larger scale than TV, is likely within this group to be more immediately useful.

Much of the problem of eradicating illiteracy in India rises out of the fact that the dropout rate at primary level is so high. Children who drop out for one reason or another lapse into illiteracy easily enough, and the process of making them literate later is not easy because internally there is by now a built-in resistance to learning. What do we do to recapture these children? There is no single or simple answer to this question since there is no single or simple answer to why they dropped out in the first instance. Where the reasons are, as in rural areas socio-economic, only an inter-ministerial attack on the problem will solve it. Within the age-group 6-11, we are told that the problem is convertible with getting girls in rural areas into school. The long—and short—term solutions are well known: convince the girls' mothers that nothing but schooling or some non-formal equivalent will give their daughters a better deal in life than their mothers had; also, that it will be easier to marry off the girls with some education than with none. Teaching in the single-teacher school must be improved and this is not just educational; it is also socio-economic. If girls from a village can grow into being its teachers, the greater part of this battle is won.

The city dropout is sometimes socio-economic, too, but is more generally explained by specific educational reasons such as colourless or downright bad and irrelevant teaching. The abolition of all tests in the first year may seem a quick way out of the problem but, like all quick ways, it is not conclusive. Cumulative ignorance merely postpones the moment of dropout; it does not eliminate dropping out. Some evaluation is necessary, so even if the child is not detained in a class or failed, he/she must be watched to assess progress. Clearly, much more money has to be invested in elementary education even if this means taking it (i.e. money) away from college and university education that is manifestly over-capitalised. And the investment in elementary education has to be supervised by State Ministers of Education who have been known in the past to divert, or to permit to be diverted, funds originally earmarked for primary education.

If we wish to be effective about bringing children within the orbit of educational opportunity, we have to be willing to invest in and to trust organisations that are committed as an article af faith to the business of education and are not content with paper reports on what they have done. Women's organisations are noticeably more committed than others, and so we have to go down in a progressive process of devolution to districts and villages to ensure that trusted voluntary organisations perform effectively within manageable areas of service. If this is planned and executed with the involvement of such voluntary agencies, we may be much nearer solving this apparently insoluble problem of elementary child education.

Not long ago I heard an American educationist who had lived and worked in India for many years allude with genuine feeling to the saddest aspect of Indian education. It is as if, he said, men and women seem never to say to themselves: 'These are our children'. In Japan and the Philippines, in the late sixties, I was most agreeably surprised by precisely this involvement that is so lacking among us. The community, so it is argued or implied there, gets the schools it deserves. The schools reflect the community.

In the big cities of India—Bombay, Calcutta, Madras, Delhi—the ambitious parent is a guarantee that educational managements will be kept on their toes. Parent-Teacher Associations vary in effectiveness, but it is generally recognised that where school and parents work together, the total educational result is heartening. And so productive has this form of cooperation been that the contagion has spread to colleges where substantial results have flowed from college-community involvement. All this, however, argues an alive and progressive community. Where the community is dormant, unaware either of its capacities or its rights, these expectations and awareness of rights have to be created. By themselves, educationists cannot create such .awareness. This is an area in which nothing but kaleidoscopic action will suffice for the attack and continued campaigning on ignorance, darkness, lethargy and the general sense of helplessness and hopelessness. So many of our committees in education are static and without result that it would be as well to call these urgent kaleidoscopic committees barefoot to signify the need for down-to-earth planning and mobility. The Barefoot Committees must consist of a teacher, a social worker, a doctor, a nurse and an administrator with the ability and the power to coordinate work and to implement decisions. Barefoot committees require to be set up in areas most resistant to bringing children to school. Here, the chief function of the committee is to bring the school to the children. The committee, in a sense, travels barefoot to the barefoot child to bring him/ her learning in an acceptable form. To prevent idealist mushroom organisations that flourish and wither in a day, we ought to resort for initiative only to those voluntary organisations that have a record of sustained and successful community service, where lines of communication have been maintained through a period of at least 20 years. The YWCA is far-flung and has been known to have dedicated field workers; also, the Ramakrishna Mission that people remember with respect. The terms on which these and other tried agencies are induced to expand their responsibilities within a compressed period of time ought to be liberalised to enable them to increase the size of their programmes and intensify their activities.

The suggestion that part-time workers be mobilised is good and likely to be effective now that women have begun a campaign for part-time paid work. Married women whose children have grown up, and whose husbands live their lives in male completeness, are anxious to find purpose and profit in life, and would therefore be willing to take on part-time work if it is steadily remunerated. Some organisation is necessary in the shape of a bureau of part-time employment to work this out, and again such work could be entrusted to a voluntary agency.

At secondary school and at college level, the problem is less one of quantity than of quality. It is at least three-sided: to make the learning process available to children of 14-17 still outside school; to make provision for good teaching through any usable media; to make education productive through effective schemes of vocationalisation.

The implementation of non-formal education from 14 upwards is so much simpler than below this age, that we need say little to persuade the public to agree with us. Since children of 14 can read easily, textbooks have to be printed on a large scale and they have to be good textbooks and inexpensive. Radio is extremely effective at this level and must be experimented with much more than has yet been done in both rural and urbal areas. Television can be used where it is available, but the problem is to find expertise in its use and the communicators must be trained for specific age-groups. Correspondence courses with contact sessions can be made to work even before 16 and certainly after it. The non-collegiate programme of education at present in existence requires to be expanded on the lines already made widely known by the Open University experiment in Britain. This has been described in books and pamphlets, discussed, clarified and re-clarified over BBC programmes and has been proven to be capable, of adaptation to developing societies in many parts of the world. Adaptation of the scheme to our needs and circumstances is essential and the scope for innovation is large. With our experience of correspondence courses, with radio instruction and television support, with the full involvement of University Departments in both school and college non-formal education, there is little doubt that such methods could be made widely and deeply effective. What is necessary is careful planning for a year, and then the careful writing of courses by coordinated expertise till no part of India that wants this sort of education is without it. What Britain has done with spectacular results, has been proved to be capable of being done. Nothing except our own lack of initiative and self-confidence stands in the way of our improving on the British example.

27

Improve Your College Library and Use It*

There are two major ways of learning:

(i) From people directly;

(ii) From books written by people, some of whom are dead.

We generally refer to the first way as teaching and being taught; to the second, as learning from books.

Even if we in India had superlatively good teachers, we would need books, for teachers draw their professional sustenance from books and, in any case, do not have sufficient time in contact with students to teach them all that students ought to know in 1975. But the fact is that we do not have, for the most part, outstanding or even very good college teachers in India, and so we are more dependent on books than societies that still have knowledgeable, curious, persistent and professional teachers at college level.

We are still not a book-buying public and books have shot up in price almost as if they had a large oil-component. So with the best will in the world, we could not buy all the books we needed. We are driven by the situation to depend on libraries, and primarily on libraries at our own place of work, i.e. college libraries.

---

* Earlier published in *New Frontiers in Education*, 1975.

What is the state of college libraries in India? I have worked for the last three years at a good women's college in New Delhi, and for the last year, at a good men's college on the Delhi University campus. 1 speak not as a professional librarian, for much as I now regret this, I have had no professional training in librarianship. I speak as a consumer, and possibly in this respect represent most people here. In neither of the colleges in which I have worked have I found conditions in the library that should exist in 1975, though the men's college has reasonable space and a very large number of books, and the women's college is working hard to improve its position in library space (at present pitifully inadequate) and to supply its deficiencies in relevant books. But it is not of space or brick-and-mortar that I wish to speak in this paper. It is of Library Services. For the library is not, in the ordinary sense, a department of an educational institution. No teaching is done in a library. The library is a service, and it is in this respect that most Indian colleges are for 1975 sadly inadequate.

A college library exists to promote learning and learning experiences through reading and through discussion, following reading. The attitudes that dominate library services in many Indian colleges today are, by a curious contradiction, more illustrative of the desire to impede, than to promote learning. One can understand that, since library grants are strictly limited, and since books are progressively more expensive, all rational steps must be taken to ensure that books are carefully used, and not destroyed, defaced, mutilated, lost or stolen. One has only to consider how long it took to win the battle of the books to reach the Open Shelf method, to see that there is among librarians a built-in resistance (of which they are barely conscious) to emptied shelves. But the function of a librarian is to ensure, and to promote the quick circulation of books. A library that is always a portrait of 'books coldly ranged on shelves' is a badly-serviced library. Books must be used, and we must take the chance of loss with naturally all reasonable precautions to keep loss, destruction and the rest down to a minimum.

We are all aware of colleges that advertise themselves in their handbooks as having a very large number of books, and their libraries live up to this description. But the number of books is only one component of a good library and, by itself, it is not a particularly important component. A college library is, or should be, a place to learn in through reading. An unweeded library of dated or irrelevant books, no matter how numerous, is not necessarily a satisfactory place to learn in, in 1975. A college library is not a museum. It never was intended for collections of first editions. Many Indian colleges provide library services for a first Honours and Pass degree and some for a Master's degree, too. But many more require students studying for an MA to use the University, in preference to the college library, and this is not unreasonable. College libraries in India have, therefore to cater primarily for students at first degree level, and for faculty engaged in teaching these students. If the tutorial system is to be worked as this much-misunderstood system should work, good library services are indispensable. One reason, though not the most important, why the tutorial system is not working everywhere, is the inadequacy of library services. In what does this inadequacy consist?

There is, in the first place, the human, professional inadequacy of many librarians. You would have thought that almost any one normal in daily association with the range and depth of learning that books in a modern library imply, would contrive to be educated through reading, largely because this is what his/her work is about. It is not asking for the impossible to expect that librarians should be better educated, in the sense of better informed, than most other people on a college campus. During my stay of a year in the State Department of Education, New York in 1964-65, I had to visit and demonstrate teaching in about 200 secondary and elementary schools of the State. The student material was, as you would expect in this most affluent part of an affluent society, outstanding. The teachers were ambitious, energetic, sometimes deeply perceptive of their students' needs. The brick-and-mortar left you wondering whether you had strayed into a millionaire's establishment or merely into an educational institution. But far and away the most impressive element in the situation was the fact that the librarian in the 200 schools (and she was generally a woman) was remarkably well-informed.

Most booksellers in India today do not know the contents of the books they press so diligently upon their customers. They have not even troubled to read the blurb that advertises the book. It is an unusual bookseller in India who can tell you what a book is about, and so advise on its purchase in preference to other comparable books. And we, inured to this state of seemingly impregnable ignorance, put up with it. But librarians are not entitled to the same indulgence since it is part of their professional function to advise readers. This advisory function is performed automatically in all good libraries in the developed world. The librarian, man or woman, even if not a profound scholar, is knowledgeable in respect of relevant books. He is, for consumer-purposes, an educated adviser; but librarians in many Indian colleges are no more aware of the connection between books and authors, subjects and authors, than their assistants at various descending levels, all of whom are generally there in body (and so within reach of the books) but contribute nothing in mind to the effectiveness of the library's services. I have become aware in recent years of a special kind of "illiteracy" that I have come, without cynicism, to expect of, and to reserve for college librarians. The notes I receive from them in answer to queries are misspelt, inaccurate and reveal deplorable ignorance on matters relating to the books they brood over in token of their proprietary rights within their domain. They are defensive about their relative obscurity on the college campus, and the fact that there is often an imperfect sympathy between faculty and themselves. Into this conflict, I will not enter, except to say that everyone, at all times, in an educational situation must, to have respect, earn it. It is not automatic: it does not follow upon an advertised status. And the librarian who today distinguished himself from his compeers, by knowing the contents of some of his books, would obtain by the sheer rarity of this accomplishment, the reverence of a faculty that regards itself as requiring to be serviced by him.

Not merely is the representative Indian college librarian not knowledgeable; he is not helpful. To point to the card index when you are asked a question that implies information not contained therein, and when someone is in a tearing hurry, is not merely obtuse; it is bad manners and the negation of professionalism. But this is what so many college librarians do. You are directed to the card index or the shelves, and these are your final court of appeal for learning. You are never given alternatives to the book you want, that may help you out of a sticky situation. And worse: you are never given the wholesome and comforting impression that the librarian will do all he can to help you.

If this is so vis-a-vis faculty, it is ten times more so in relation to students. For between college librarians and students, there appears to be a state of unpeaceful coexistence in which each regards the other as his natural enemy. The librarian resents the truculence of the student; the student, the persistent unhelpfulness of the librarian. And valuable time, that should be spent in cooperation to promote learning, is wasted in fruitless recrimination and unnecessary suspicion, accusation and hostility—just the climate in which learning withers and decays.

The employment as librarians of people who are much less generally-well educated than faculty, and are of attitude resentful towards students, tells against making the library what a college library should be: a refuge against controversy, a source of quiet re-freshing and private self-confidence. An educated librarian in such a situation would provide the academic poise that is necessary to advise where advice is expected. This degree of educational self-confidence would also possibly supply an element of creativity that is at present, if my experience be general, wholly missing from the college library in India. The librarian is not merely there to respond to a request for advice on books; he is also there to create progressively services within the library that promote learning. This, he may not be able to do single-handed. He will need to work in close association with faculty and students, but only a professionally-equipped librarian could and would assist as a matter of course the sort of learning experience I have in mind.

The librarian in most college libraries is uneducated and badly informed. In the second place, most college librarians do not, as a matter of course, invest in multiple copies of the same important books. Yet this is now essential for seminars and is clearly possible with comparatively inexpensive paperbacks within our reach. Here, again, is a deeply-entrenched prejudice. Paperbacks, we are told parrotwise, do not endure and so the librarian will not buy them. But paperbacks can easily be bound, and in the present state of the book-market, there is really no alternative to the large-scale purchase of paperbacks to promote the learning experience, at the same time, among a large number of students.

What is this learning experience that requires the close association of librarians, faculty and students? I speak out of direct experience initially in India, the United Kingdom, the United States— and back again in India at college level.

Most forward-looking organisations in India, and among these I include the UGC, have seen through the lecture system, have deplored the manner in which it works its wonders to perform frequently even in 1975 with dictated notes repeated from year to year, have recognised that students are bored with the performance of most lecturers and that some student indiscipline is directly attributable to this boredom. They have, moreover, suggested alternative methods and have strongly recommended experiments in new methods of learning. I have observed that, where attendance or some measure of attendance is compulsory, good students (and not merely drifters) will attend classes to put in their quota of attendance, and then quite scientifically stay away. Outstanding lecturers who have something new to say, or something old to say in a new, relevant and penetrating way may possibly not lack a student-audience. But by and large lecturers know just how poor they are by consulting their student attendance registers. The lecture system for ordinary people is a poor one: only outstanding teachers can beat it, and it is time that we were willing to see this. What are the alternatives to the lecture?

Seminars and tutorials are alternatives, but a third alternative that has been tried out and worked in certain pre-arranged situations is worth considering. The Library Seminar is an experiment in the learning process for, through it, a group of homogeneous and able students learn individually and collectively through a book and in a library. The perfect size for such a group is ten, though in special cases, this could be reduced to eight or stretched to twelve. I have guided a library seminar with as many as 25 secondary school teachers of about the same level of excellence, and this worked, but only because the teachers were all engaged, through a book, in an evaluation of their own teaching in a common situation. Ordinarily, 25 is too large for an effective library seminar.

It is essential to the success of this method that the participants shall be intellectually homogeneous. This does not mean that they need be alike in most respects. A wide range of temperament and talent can, and should preferably exist in each group, for variety intensifies interest and stimulates growth. But they must be of approximately the same perceptive ability; they must be analytic; they must be about as articulate as one another, though even here there is room for varying degrees of articulateness. Students from different years of the same course, and in different disciplines may participate in the same library seminar. Inter-disciplinary participation is frequently very salutary.

The library seminar works round a book and in a library. The book must be wisely chosen and there must be multiple copies of it for simultaneous use. The book must interest the age-group involved; it must provide scope for discussion; it must be capable of being related to other thought-provoking books in the library; it must stimulate the thinking process. It follows that a book concerned primarily with adventure, pure narrative, incontestable truth is not ideal, Many of the classics fail to provide outstanding library seminars because they no longer stimulate discussion or interest. Not long ago a group with which I was associated, was asked to demonstrate a library seminar on *Great Expectations* for the benefit of a school's 11th class that had studied the book as a text. The group complied but was not enthusiastic. Why? Because Dickens' novel on the dangers of choosing to be a "gentleman" over a gentle man no longer cuts any ice. It has dated in idea, and though it still provides fun at school level, is not relevant to the life of college students in India. Groups of Honours students with whom I have worked for a year have conducted library seminars on *A Passage to India, Animal Farm, Howards End* and *Lord of the Flies*. All these are suitable because they are books of ideas that stimulate thought, provoke discussion and lead students to explore libraries further in support of points of view.

In the mechanics of the library seminar there are two factors of overriding importance: atmosphere and leadership. The venue must be a library, for it is the library that supplies atmosphere. The library seminar, as its name implies, is book-dominated, but it is not textbook dominated. It represents a wide variety of books on the same subject, a variety of books by the same author, places author and critic side by side, teaches students to scrutinise the printed word, to assess, to criticise, to understand and to judge for themselves. In this world, excellence and mediocrity both proclaim themselves.

The seminar takes place in a library, but a library cordoned off from the general reader while the seminar is in session.

The seminar is designed for its participants who sit round a table and are left to uninterrupted discussion and discovery, frequently rising to pick a book off the shelves as they discuss for a period of generally two hours. They work in a relaxed atmosphere and may drink tea or coffee and eat a snack as they talk. Towards the end of the period, the discussion is thrown open by the leader of the group to observers who may be present, but have not participated.

Because the library seminar is a form of student government, leadership is of the first importance. The leader initiates discussion on a book that every participant has read, studied and inwardly digested. No summary of content is therefore necessary. A faculty member associated with the group has, in the previous two to three weeks, structured the discussion in association with the group. There is therefore something like a chart or circumscribed area within which discussion takes place; it does not range too widely. The faculty member is present throughout the preliminary sessions as well as at the final presentation. He/she may intervene to keep discussion on the rails or to prevent disproportionate emphasis being given to a single point or to stimulate discussion that has tended to get bogged down between two or three of the more articulate participants. But he/she is outside the group. Far and away the most attractive aspect of the library seminar to students at college level is this aspect of self-government and the evolution of leaders.

All participants in library seminars are able students and potential leaders i.e. they are intellectual, able to analyse and generally articulate about ideas. They are invariably readers, people who go naturally to libraries and who read for pleasure. The assumption, therefore, is that we are dealing with people given to connecting ideas in books, who do not take the printed word for law, who criticise what they read and reach independent conclusions. 'The library seminar offers them the chance to measure themselves against others of comparable ability. Leadership automatically emerges.

There are as many kinds of leadership as there are numbers of participants. The best leaders are those who read wisely, think quickly and are aware of others' points of view. They are not necessarily deeply scholarly, but they respect scholarship that they recognise. They tend to relate thinking and reading to living. The success of a library seminar is frequently directly correlated with the quality of leadership found for it.

Participants are told that in this method of learning, each will in general travel at his own pace. No debating points will be allowed and, even where partisanship occurs, it will not be of a purely verbal kind. The participants may agree to differ. A time limit implies that discussion must stop even where agreement has not been reached. The purpose of the library seminar is clear thinking, individually and collectively, not consensus.

Our curriculum for a first degree assumes that such books as *A Passage to India* will be taught and learnt in the course of a semester. *Howards End,* that is comparable to the *Passage,* took precisely three weeks to master through a library seminar. A group of ten students who worked in association with me, took two weeks to read the book on their own initiative. In the course of this period, they met me three times, discussed the book among themselves and with me on the basis of a structured list of questions, that I had drawn up for them. They then went into public session in the presence of an audience of informed adults a week later. Two library seminars on the same book have both proved extremely successful. The second was undertaken to demonstrate the method to a sister-college in Simla with the encouraging result that this college has now adopted the method and is using it with adaptations. The Television Centre at Delhi was interested in the experiment and televised an abridged version of it in the course of 1974. This elicited interested comment from a wide circle of educationists. Asked if they were ready to sit for an examination on the book, every single participant was willing to do so. All claimed that the library seminar had helped them to understand the *Passage* and E.M. Forster.

In every library seminar the participants have been given evaluation sheets in which they express themselves candidly. The method is naturally experimental, works where the essential conditions for its success are realised, and not where they are absent. Follow-up is necessary in a library or a classroom. Those who participate act as leavening in any follow-up session. The participants are stimulated to read other books by the same author or books by different authors on similar themes. And the library comes in time to be a living place. Books take on the character of living friends. They are not lecturers performing to order on a pre-arranged platform or pedestal. They are associates in learning, at par with the learner. To be remembered, they have to be memorable through the printed word. They stand or fall on merit.

What has the library and the librarian to do to make this method of learning a success? To cooperate at every stage with the faculty member planning the seminar, and to cooperate at similar stages with the participants who need his help. This help can be given only if the librarian truly knows his library, the contents of books, the general contour of what eminent authors have written, in short, if he is well-informed on bibliographies, on relevant recent writing, the books that he has himself been instrumental in buying for the library over which he presides.

At the Jesus and Mary College, New Delhi, we have planned, on a voluntary basis, an Advanced Programme in English Literature that will be introduced in the next academic year. This programme has, as its objective, the achievement of a deep understanding of Literature in English among students interested in, and capable of attaining high excellence through courses in depth in selected areas that are not ordinarily covered in the curriculum for the BA degree of the Delhi University. The programme sets out to create and to stimulate an interest in (i) The Contemporary Novel in English, covering the period 1930-1975 (ii) Poetic Form and (iii) A Century of Drama (1875-1975). In administering it, the Department of English at the college has, of its own initiative, hammered out a curriculum for which it will need a well-serviced library. By and by, and as funds permit, we will need to have recordings and video-tapes to help us achieve the many-faceted understanding of literature that we have made our objective. Till we can equip ourselves, we will borrow from organisations that are willing to lend to us. The important thing, however, is to develop, as we go along, our own college library, so that sooner than later, it can service all the innovation in learning that such a programme implies.

In this process it is possible that both faculty/library will come to see themselves for what they are: guides to progressive learning rather than repositaries of unchanging knowledge. We may even go a step further: in developing the three courses I have mentioned, we may come collectively to impart to learning, that element of creativity, that more than anything else, makes work worth doing, and life worth living within an educational community.